Frog Math: Predict, Ponder, Play

teacher's guide

Grades
Kindergarten–3

Skills
Observing, Cooperating, Logical Thinking, Problem-Solving, Collecting and Interpreting Data, Sorting and Classifying, Using Geometric Vocabulary, Noticing and Articulating Patterns, Graphing, Estimating, Predicting, Developing and Testing Strategies

Concepts
Literature and Art Connections to Mathematics, Classification, Number, Place Value, Pattern Recognition, Estimation, Probability and Statistics

Science Themes
Diversity & Unity, Models & Simulations, Systems & Interactions, Structure, Scale

Mathematics Strands
Logic and Language, Geometry, Number, Statistics and Probability, Discrete Mathematics, Pattern

Nature of Science and Mathematics
Cooperative Efforts, Real-Life Applications, Theory-Based and Testable, Interdisciplinary

Time
Six 45–60 minute sessions, plus possible follow-up sessions

by
Jaine Kopp

Great Explorations in Math and Science (GEMS)
Lawrence Hall of Science
University of California at Berkeley

Illustrations
Lisa Klofkorn

Cover Illustration
Lisa Haderlie Baker

Photographs
Richard Hoyt

Cover Design
Nona Pepino

Lawrence Hall of Science, University of California, Berkeley, CA 94720.

Publication of *Frog Math* was made possible by a grant from the Hewlett Packard Company Foundation. The GEMS project and the Lawrence Hall of Science greatly appreciate this support.

Initial support for the origination and publication of the GEMS series was provided by the A.W. Mellon Foundation and the Carnegie Corporation of New York. GEMS has also received support from the McDonnell-Douglas Foundation and the McDonnell-Douglas Employees Community Fund, the Hewlett Packard Company Foundation, and the people at Chevron USA. GEMS also gratefully acknowledges the contribution of word processing equipment from Apple Computer, Inc. This support does not imply responsibility for statements or views expressed in publications of the GEMS program. Under a grant from the National Science Foundation, GEMS Leader's Workshops have been held across the country. For further information on GEMS leadership opportunities, or to receive a publication brochure and the *GEMS Network News*, please contact GEMS at the address and phone number below.

International Standard Book Number: 0-924886-02-1

COMMENTS WELCOME

Great Explorations in Math and Science (GEMS) is an ongoing curriculum development project. GEMS guides are revised periodically, to incorporate teacher comments and new approaches. We welcome your criticisms, suggestions, helpful hints, and any anecdotes about your experience presenting GEMS activities. Your suggestions will be reviewed each time a GEMS guide is revised. Please send your comments to: GEMS Revisions, c/o Lawrence Hall of Science, University of California, Berkeley, CA 94720. The phone number is (510) 642-7771.

Great Explorations in Math and Science (GEMS) Program

The Lawrence Hall of Science (LHS) is a public science center on the University of California at Berkeley campus. LHS offers a full program of activities for the public, including workshops and classes, exhibits, films, lectures, and special events. LHS is also a center for teacher education and curriculum research and development.

Over the years, LHS staff have developed a multitude of activities, assembly programs, classes, and interactive exhibits. These programs have proven to be successful at the Hall and should be useful to schools, other science centers, museums, and community groups. A number of these guided-discovery activities have been published under the Great Explorations in Math and Science (GEMS) title, after an extensive refinement process that includes classroom testing of trial versions, modifications to ensure the use of easy-to-obtain materials, and carefully written and edited step-by-step instructions and background information to allow presentation by teachers without special background in mathematics or science.

Staff

Glenn T. Seaborg, **Principal Investigator**
Jacqueline Barber, **Director**
Kimi Hosoume, **Assistant Director**
Cary Sneider, **Curriculum Specialist**
Carolyn Willard, **GEMS Centers Coordinator**
Laura Tucker, **GEMS Workshop Coordinator**
Terry Cort, **GEMS Workshop Representative**
Katharine Barrett, Kevin Beals, Ellen Blinderman, Beatrice Boffen, Gigi Dornfest, John Erickson, Jaine Kopp, Laura Lowell, Linda Lipner, Debra Sutter, Rebecca Tilley, **Staff Development Specialists**
Jan M. Goodman, **Mathematics Consultant**
Cynthia Eaton, **Administrative Coordinator**
Karen Milligan, **Distribution Coordinator**
Felicia Roston, **Shipping Coordinator**
George Kasarjian, **Shipping Assistant**
Bryan Burd, **Shipping Assistant**
Stephanie Van Meter, **Program Assistant**
Lisa Haderlie Baker, **Art Director**
Carol Bevilacqua, Rose Craig, Lisa Klofkorn, **Designers**
Lincoln Bergman, **Principal Editor**
Carl Babcock, **Senior Editor**
Florence Stone, **Assistant Editor**
Kay Fairwell, **Principal Publications Coordinator**
Larry Gates, Lisa Ghahraman, Alisa Sramala, Mary Yang, **Staff Assistants**

Contributing Authors

Jacqueline Barber
Katharine Barrett
Kevin Beals
Lincoln Bergman
Celia Cuomo
Linda De Lucchi
Gigi Dornfest
Jean Echols
Philip Gonsalves
Jan M. Goodman
Alan Gould
Kimi Hosoume
Susan Jagoda
Jaine Kopp
Linda Lipner
Laura Lowell
Larry Malone
Cary I. Sneider
Debra Sutter
Jennifer Meux White
Carolyn Willard

Reviewers

We would like to thank the following educators who reviewed, tested, or coordinated the reviewing of this series of GEMS materials in manuscript and draft form. Their critical comments and recommendations, based on presentation of these activities in classrooms nationwide, contributed significantly to these GEMS publications. Their participation in the review process does not necessarily imply endorsement of the GEMS program or responsibility for statements or views expressed in these publications. Their role is an invaluable one, and their feedback is carefully recorded and integrated as appropriate into the publications. Thank You!

ARIZONA
Coordinator: Richard Clark

Manzanita Elementary School, Phoenix
Linda K. Carter
Terry Dalton
Deborah S. Miller
Sandy Stanley

CALIFORNIA

Huntington Beach GEMS Center
Coordinator: Susan Spoeneman

College View Elementary School, Huntington Beach
Marshall Baldwin
Martha Deal
Gretchen McKay
Linda Koch Mosier
Kathy O'Steen

Agnes L. Smith School, Huntington Beach
Mary Dyer
Margaret E. Hayes
Janis D. Liss
Judy Miskanic

Anaheim City School District

Loama and Marshall Elementary Schools
Judy Swank

Palm Lane and Jefferson Elementary Schools
Peggy Okimoto

San Francisco Bay Area
Coordinator: Cynthia Ashley

Columbus Intermediate School, Berkeley
Susan DeWitt
Jose Franco
Katherine Lunine
Richard Silberg

Glassbrooke Elementary School, Hayward
Marianne Camp
Mary Davis

Henderson Elementary School, Benicia
Cathy Larripa
Sheila Ruhl
Carol A. Pilling
Barry Wofsy

Hoover Elementary School, Oakland
Margaret Coleman
Wanda Price

Oxford Elementary School, Berkeley
Anita Baker
Joseph Brulenski
Carol Bennett-Simmons
Sharon Kelly
Judy Kono
Janet Levinson

Park Day School, Oakland
Karen Corzan
Joan Wright-Albertini

Steffan Manor School, Vallejo
Don Baer
Sheila Himes
Annie Howard
Anna Reid
Bob Schneider
Monica A. Spini
Randy Stava

Stoneman Elementary School, Pittsburg
Varan Garro
Ann Quinlan-Miani
Linda Pineda
Joan Shelton

Travis Elementary School, Vallejo
Joyce Corcoran
Janet Matthews

Windrush School, El Cerrito
Margo Lillig
Barbara Minton
Louise Perry
Hillary Smith
Martha Vlahos

GEORGIA
Coordinator: Judy Dennison

Seaborn Lee Elementary School, Atlanta
- Linda Keller
- Kay Likins
- Cindy Riley
- Christine Ann Walker

KENTUCKY
Coordinator: Dee Moore

Dunn Elementary School, Louisville
- Claudia George
- Pam Kleine-Kracht
- Cynthia Macshmeyer
- Judith R. Stubbs

Coleridge-Taylor Elementary School, Louisville
- Nancy Benge
- Vicki Bumann
- Andrea Lentz
- Ruth Ann Little

NEW YORK
Coordinator: Stan Wegrzynowski

D'Youville Porter Campus School, Buffalo
- Barbara Johnson
- Marikay Reville Loftus
- Lynette Parker
- Deborah Ann Rudyk
- Francine R. Shea

Science Magnet School #59, Buffalo
- Sue M. Combs
- Janet E. Lawrence
- Sharon Pikul
- Gail M. Russo

OREGON
Coordinator, Ann Kennedy

Cedaroak Park Elementary School, West Linn
- Dennis E. Adams
- Sue Foster
- Jaylin Redden-Hefty
- Cheri Weaver

TEXAS
Coordinator: Karen Ostlund

Deepwood Elementary School, Round Rock
- Lana Culver
- Sara Field
- Myra P. Fowler
- Karen Lena
- M. Mercado
- Sherry Wilkison

WASHINGTON
Coordinators: Scott Stowell and Diana D'Aboy

Arlington Elementary School, Spokane
- Esther C. Baker
- Pauline Eggleston
- Linda Graham
- JoAnn Lamb
- Sue Rodman
- Dorothy Schultheis
- Becky Sherwood
- Gayle Vaughn

Bemiss Elementary School, Spokane
- Ethel Barstow
- Lee Anne Fowler
- Bettie Maron
- Cathy Mitchell

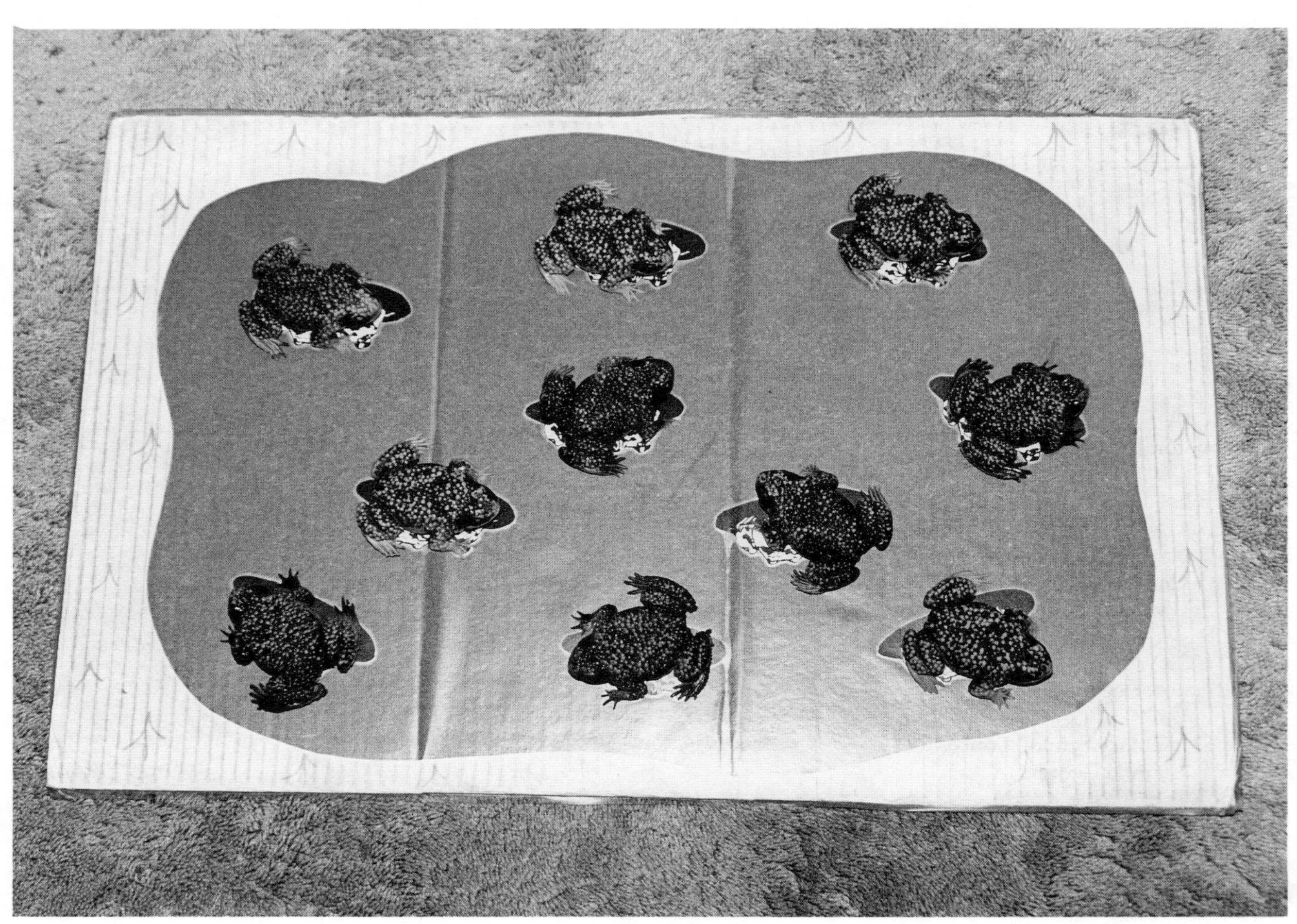

Table of Contents

Acknowledgments

When Jaine Kopp (the author of this *Frog Math* teacher's guide) first arrived at the Lawrence Hall of Science in October 1989, she discovered an abundance of little green frogs on the math shelves. Knowing that these little critters would be of high interest to young students, she used them to develop "Frog Guesstimation" and the "Frog Pond Game." Meanwhile, Linda Lipner, Director of the Mathematics Education Department, began using "The Lost Button" story as a literary springboard for button-related math activities. Connected by the frog motif (and many mathematics strands) the idea for a GEMS guide evolved. The button activities were further developed for the guide and the "Hop to the Pond" game was adapted from a game that Jan Goodman of the Mathematics Education Department created. The author is very appreciative of the support and insight that both Linda and Jan have provided as the guide was developed.

The author would also like to thank Carolyn Willard who served as her GEMS "buddy" throughout the process of creating the trial versions and writing the guide. Her support and eye for detail were invaluable. Additional thanks goes to Jan Goodman for assistance with the computer graphics for the "Place Value" and "Hop to the Pond" boards. And a big round of applause and many thanks go to Lisa Haderlie Baker for her delightful and whimsical cover illustration that captures the essence of *Frog Math*.

We would especially like to thank the children in Lina Prairie's class, at Downer Elementary School in Richmond, California, for their enthusiasm and contributions to the refinement of the activities. Special thanks as well to the children at Park Day School in Oakland who grace the photographs in this guide.

Finally, the GEMS project thanks all the GEMS reviewers and their students throughout the country who leapfrogged right into *Frog Math*, and through their valuable feedback made their own special contributions to these "ribbiting" math activities.

Introduction

Charm your class with some enchanting frogs that turn into mathematics principles at the touch of a student's hand! Your students will learn by "leaps and bounds," gaining skills such as observing, predicting, describing, classifying, estimating, recording data, and using logic and probability to develop thinking strategies. Frogs and mathematics hop along together in this series of engaging activities, along with literature, art and writing, and lots of fun!

Students begin by listening to a story called "The Lost Button" from Arnold Lobel's popular book *Frog and Toad Are Friends.* A cooperative, free exploration of colorful and differing buttons in this first session prepares the students for sorting and classifying buttons in Session 2. In Session 3, students create unique paper buttons and organize them on a class graphing grid. In Session 4, frogs hop back in a big way in a series of non-competitive estimation and counting activities. In Sessions 5 and 6, students play two delightful frog games that develop logical thinking skills and introduce probability and statistics. All of the sessions in *Frog Math* include many important student learning objectives. These objectives are noted in the "Overviews" to each session.

As more states and districts implement new programs in activity-based science and mathematics, units such as those in the GEMS series are often used to construct effective and exciting curricula. In California, for example, Frog Math *has been selected by leading mathematics educators as a recommended unit. This means these educators have endorsed the content and approach of* Frog Math *as an excellent way to bring guided discovery, interdisciplinary learning in mathematics into the classroom as an alternative to traditional textbooks. The strong connection made in this guide between literature and mathematics deepens this educational effectiveness while giving it broad appeal to teachers and students.*

Although *Frog Math* works well for all primary students, you'll find that you will occasionally need to adjust the activities to suit the maturity and experience of your students. We have included important modifications of the activities for kindergarten students at the end of each session. At times, you may be able to do the activity with your kindergarten students as it is written. However, there may be places where it is particularly important to use the modifications, as in the case of Session 4, which includes a lima bean estimation activity for older students, and Session 6, where there is an additional game for older students. In addition, we have indicated adaptations for second and third grade students, as suggested by teachers. In Session 2, for example, you will find more independent and sophisticated classification alternatives for older students. Suggestions for additional activities are given in the "Going Further" sections for each session. All the activities are designed to be flexible so you can adapt them to the abilities and needs of your students. One thing's for sure—**all** your students will love *Frog Math*!

Student sheets and gameboard masters are included at the end of the session in which they are needed. Additional, removable copies of these, as well as several enlarged versions, are included at the end of the guide, for your convenience.

A frog in a pond went to play
A game with a friend one fine day
As they pondered and thought
Both were hoppily taught
Mathematics a funderful way!

Button Template

Time Frame

For each session there is some initial preparation time needed to make nonconsumable materials that can be used again each time you teach *Frog Math*. These materials include several items, such as a place value board and a graphing grid, that many teachers also find very helpful for other mathematics lessons during the course of the year. We have listed this one-time-only preparation time first, with an asterisk, and then estimated the time needed for set-up on the day of the activity.

Session 1: Materials Preparation: 45 minutes*
Set-Up Time: 10-15 minutes
Classroom Activity: 45–60 minutes

Session 2: Materials Preparation: 45 minutes*
Set-Up Time: 10-15 minutes
Classroom Activity: 45–60 minutes

Session 3: Materials Preparation: 45 minutes*
Set-Up Time: 10-15 minutes
Classroom Activity: 45–60 minutes

Session 4: Materials Preparation: 30 minutes*
Set-Up Time: 10-15 minutes
Classroom Activity: 45–60 minutes

Session 5: Materials Preparation: 45 minutes*
Set-Up Time: 10 minutes
Classroom Activity: 45–60 minutes

Session 6: Materials Preparation: 45 minutes*
Set-Up Time: 10 minutes
Classroom Activity: 45–60 minutes

Session 1 : The Lost Button Story

Overview

In this first activity, your students hear an engaging story, "The Lost Button" by Arnold Lobel. In the story, Frog and Toad go on a long walk. At the end of the walk, Toad notices—much to his dismay—that he has lost a button. As Frog and Toad retrace their steps in search of Toad's button, they find many buttons, but none of them is the one Toad lost. Literature meets mathematics as your students discover the **attributes** of the missing button. It is a white, four-holed, big, round, thick button! And Toad does find it—on the floor, back in his home!

After the story, the students get their hands on some real buttons! Working in pairs, students thoroughly enjoy this opportunity to freely explore the buttons. It is very important for them to have this time to investigate in the fun ways they choose. Although some teams may begin to observe the attributes of their buttons at this time, there is no formal task yet; all students, through play, gain a great deal of information about the buttons, no matter how they investigate them. If students have plenty of free exploration time now, they will be better able to focus and cooperate with each other in Session 2, when they are given more specific challenges.

This first activity encourages students to: connect literature and mathematics; make their own discoveries in an open-ended setting; strengthen oral language and listening skills; develop attribute vocabulary words; use concrete materials to increase observation skills; and work cooperatively.

What You Need

For the class:

- ❐ 1 copy of the *Frog and Toad Are Friends* book by Arnold Lobel
- ❐ 1 light blue felt board—24" x 18"
- ❐ 1 piece of white felt—12" x 18"
- ❐ 1 piece of black felt—6" x 6"
- ❐ 1 hole puncher
- ❐ 1 pair scissors
- ❐ white glue

For each pair of students:

- ❐ 1 collection of 40–50 buttons, as diverse as possible in size, color, shape, number of holes, texture.
- ❐ 1 paper cup (or any container large enough to hold 40–50 buttons)
- ❐ paper and drawing implements (for 2nd and 3rd grade students only)

Getting Ready

1. At least a month before the activity, have your students begin to create a collection of buttons. A sample letter to parents requesting donations is included on page 69. In addition to the children's buttons, you may want to purchase some unusual buttons for the collection. **Sources for buttons include discount fabric stores and educational catalogs, some of which are listed on page 71.** The collection can continue to grow throughout the unit and then will be available for the next time you teach these activities.

2. Obtain a copy of the *Frog and Toad Are Friends* book by Arnold Lobel. Read "The Lost Button" story to familiarize yourself with the storyline and to note the points at which you will use the felt buttons in conjunction with the story. (See #2 in "Reading and Exploring," page 8. You may want to place "post-its" in the book in order to mark the six points in the story at which you display the felt buttons to the class.)

3. Purchase or make a felt board. To make a felt board:

   a. Cut a 18"x 24" piece of heavy, corrugated cardboard or foam core board.

   b. Cut a 22"x 28" piece of light blue felt.

c. Place the felt down on a flat surface. Put the board you are using on top of the felt so it is centered. There should be a 2" border of felt around the board.

d. Wrap the borders of felt around to the back of the board, one side at a time, starting with a 24" long side. Wrap that side and staple it down. Wrap the second 24" side, pull the felt taut and staple. Continue, taking care to adjust the felt before stapling.

4. Cut out felt buttons as follows:

Alternately, one teacher used construction paper for the buttons and displayed them in a pocket chart.

- 1 large, black, round button with one hole
- 1 small, white, round button with two holes
- 1 small, white, round button with four holes
- 1 large, white, square button with four holes
- 5 large, white, round buttons with four holes

The *large*, round buttons are 4" in diameter and the *small* are 2 3/4" in diameter. The square button is 4" in length. The *thick* button is made by gluing four of the large, white, round, buttons with four holes together.

5. On the day you present the lesson, gather the book, felt board and the felt buttons. Stack the buttons in the order that you will display them as follows:

- black button with one hole (*TOP*)
- small button with two holes
- small button with four holes
- square button with four holes
- thin button with four holes
- thick button with four holes (*BOTTOM*)

6. For each pair of students, fill one cup with 40–50 buttons so that each cup has a wide variety of buttons, including various sizes, colors, shapes, numbers of holes, textures, and thicknesses. If the students will first be gathered away from their desks, you may place the buttons at their desks for pairs of students. Otherwise, have the cups ready to distribute after you read the story.

7. If you have second and third grade students, decide whether you will do the Button Factory closing activity. If you plan to do that activity, you'll need to have blank sheets of paper and crayons or colored markers ready for quick distribution.

Reading and Exploring

1. Gather the students on the rug or a group area so that they can all easily see the felt board. Have your stack of six felt buttons out of the children's view, but within your reach. Tell the students that they are going to begin today's mathematics class with a story. Hold up the *Frog and Toad* book. Take a few minutes to hear comments that the children may have. Introduce the story "The Lost Button" to the children.

2. Begin reading the story. Stop at each of the following six points, and place the appropriate felt button on the felt board:

1) When Frog finds the first button and shouts, "Here is your button!" put the **large, black, round, one-holed felt button** up on the felt board. Ask, "What color is the button Frog found?" [Black]

2) Continue reading until the sparrow offers a button. Then put the **small, round, white, two-holed felt button** on the felt board, and ask the children what color the button is. [White]

3) Read on until Frog finds the next button. Place the **small, round, white, four-holed felt button** on the felt board. Ask the class, "How many holes does this button have?" [Four]

4) When Raccoon comes along and offers another button,place the **large, square, white four-holed felt button** on the felt board. Ask what shape the button is. [Square]

5) When Frog finds a button at the river, place the **large, round, white, four-holed felt button** on the felt board. Ask the children if they think that this button belongs to Toad. [Thumbs up for yes and thumbs down for no.] Then ask what they think Toad will say when he sees the button. ["That is not my button."]

6) Continue reading until Toad gets back to his home and finds his button. Read the description. Ask the children if they can picture Toad's button. Put the **large, white, round, four-holed, thick felt button** on the felt board. Go over the button's attributes with the children by asking how many holes it has, whether it's thick or thin, and so on.

3. Finish reading the story. You may want to expand upon the story with a few questions, such as, "How do you think Toad feels at the end of the story?" "Has anyone ever lost something?" Allow for as much discussion as time and interest permit.

The question about items the children have lost may evolve into a lengthy discussion. You may want to consider saving this for a later period and following up that discussion with a writing activity. (See Going Further #5, page 13.)

4. Focus the children's attention on the felt buttons. Ask for their observations about the buttons. If necessary, ask specific questions to help guide their observations, such as:

> *How many have one hole?/two holes?/four holes?*
>
> *How many are large?/small?*
>
> *How many are round?/square?*
>
> *How many buttons are there in all?*

5. Tell the class they are going to investigate some real buttons. Let them know they will work in pairs. Each pair will have a cup of buttons to share. Pairs should carefully pour the buttons out of the cup. Then they will work together to find out all they can about the buttons. If your students have not had experience working in pairs, it may be a good idea to spend a minute or two modeling ways to share the buttons and work in a cooperative way.

As students are investigating the real buttons, you may want to suggest that they look for Toad's lost button. At the end of the exploration time, gather all the buttons that they selected and determine which one is the closest to the description of Toad's lost button.

6. Give the children 10–15 minutes of **free** exploration with the buttons. This first opportunity for your students to examine and manipulate the buttons as they choose is essential in the learning process.

7. As children work with the buttons, circulate and ask what they have noticed or are discovering about their buttons. This lets you informally assess the students' knowledge of attributes. Many children will not make any connection between their buttons and the attributes of the buttons in the story. That is fine! It will happen later on.

8. Use your usual signal to get the children's attention. Ask for their observations about the buttons. As they report their findings, generate a list of words that describe the buttons. They may observe the colors, textures, materials from which the buttons are made, number of holes, size, and function of the button. This discussion provides a wonderful opportunity to introduce children to the word ***shank***. A shank is a loop-shaped projection on the back of a solid button by which the button can be sewn onto fabric.

9. Choose the closing game(s) below that is (are) the most appropriate for your students, their abilities, and the amount of time available at the end of the session:

A. The "**Button Up**" game (grades 1 and 2).

- Invite students to select one favorite button from their button pile. Have them put the remaining buttons back into the cup. Collect the cups. Tell students that you are going to play the "Button Up" game, and that they will use their favorite button to play the game.

- Explain that each student will stand or stay seated depending upon the button attribute that you call out. Practice briefly to demonstrate the rules. Say "**Large buttons**: button up!" Have students who are standing hold their buttons up. Then use another attribute: "**Two holes**: button up!" Explain that some of the students with large buttons sit down now. Because two-holed buttons are now "up," only those students with large, two-holed buttons will continue to stand, while other children with small and medium-sized two-holed buttons will now stand up as well. There is only one attribute "up" at a time.

Many teachers have suggested that students simply raise their arms and hold up their buttons (or hold their arms down) according to the button's attributes, instead of standing and sitting.

- Continue the game and include a variety of attributes such as color, shape, texture, thickness and what material the button is made from. Ask the students if they can name an attribute that will allow everyone to stand up *or* have everyone sit down. You may want to have students take turns leading the game. (As a challenge for older students *after* they are proficient playing the game, alter "Button Up!" so there are two attributes necessary to stand up. For example, say, "**Large, red buttons**: button up!" or "**Shiny, shank buttons**, button up!")

- Depending on the time available after the game is completed, have students either get another cup of buttons with the same partner for additional free exploration, or help with clean up.

B. The "**Button Factory**" game (grades 2 and 3)

Depending upon your time schedule and student interest, you could consider saving the "Button Factory" game for another day. Some teachers found that the learning experience can be enhanced when the game is played in a subsequent session.

• Explain the game in the following way: Tell your class that you are a shirt designer and need buttons for all your shirts. After each shirt is designed, you call the Button Factory to order the right buttons for your shirts. The button must be described in great detail so that the button manufacturers can make the buttons exactly right for the shirts. Have the students pretend that they work in the Button Factory. As you describe this button, the students' job is to draw the button according to your specifications.

• Have a fancy button hidden in your hand. Describe this button, saying that you need it manufactured. For example: "I'd like a large button shaped like a square. (*Pause after each attribute to give students time to draw.*) The button needs to have three holes (*pause*). The button is yellow in the middle with purple around the edges (perimeter)." Ask students to hold up their pictures of the button you described. Thank the button makers, and tell them that you'll order plenty of these buttons because they will look great on your designer shirts.

• Tell students that they will now work in pairs. Have each student select one favorite button from the button pile and keep it hidden from her partner. Ask partners to put the remaining buttons back into the cups. The students will take turns being the shirt designer (who describes the button) and the Button Factory staff artist (who draws the buttons). Remind them that the goal is to describe the button so well that the Button Factory artist can draw the button exactly. The person describing watches as the artist draws so that she can give as many verbal clues as are necessary to help her partner draw an accurate picture.

10. Ask students to check at home for any unusual buttons to add to the class collection. Of course, they will need to make sure that bringing in an unusual button is okay with their parents.

Going Further

MY BUTTON
My button has alot of writting on it.
It is round and meituim sized button.
It is black and white.
It has two holes on it.

1. Have the buttons available to the students during free play time for further independent investigations.

2. Make a class book of the students' favorite buttons.

a. For their book, first grade students can use the word list to complete the "frame" sentence, "My button is________." They can do this several times to write their button's description. For example, *My button is red. My button is oval (or large, or bumpy, etc.).* In this book, the description and picture of the button can go on the same page. Have students make their pictures of the buttons large. Such a book is easy to read and helps review button attributes.

b. In second and third grade, have students write descriptions of their buttons on one side of a sheet of paper. On the reverse side of the paper, they draw a picture of their button. Encourage them to make big drawings. Put the pages of the book together so that the description of the button is on the front side of each page. This allows children the opportunity to imagine each button as they read the description. Then they turn the page and compare the drawing of the button to the button they imagined.

Scan8#
My Botton is round Gliter, Gold, four holds, Meadem size Button, with wood in the hole and it's made out of meadle

3. Play a Lost Button game. Have 6–8 students select a special button without the other students seeing. Students give the buttons to you. Spread those buttons—along with several others, including one that you have selected—on the felt board. Gather students around the felt board so that they can see all the buttons. Tell students that you have lost a button and ask for their assistance in finding it. Tell them that you will describe the button. As soon as they think they know which button it is, have them raise their hands. Demonstrate how to describe your button. For example, *I lost my button. It is round. It is a shank. It is shiny. It is metal. It has a checkerboard on it.* When most hands are up, ask for a volunteer to find your lost button. After it is identified, leave

Lost Button Attributes

My name is Siena.
Help me find my lost button!! Here's what it looks like:

1. its white
2. With gray a brown pookadots.
3. Four hools.
4. Shiney on one side
5. reel white on one side
6. Shiney White on the other side
7.
8.

Can you find my button. Therese
My button is square.
My button is red.
My button has a cross.
My button has 4-holes.
My button is big.

it on the felt board. Then have a student take a turn describing his lost button. Continue until all students have had a turn. Another version of this game is similar to Twenty Questions. Instead of the person who lost the button describing it, other students ask questions about the lost button until they find it.

4. Button Count: Have students estimate the total number of buttons that they have on their clothing. (No need to record estimates.) Give students a moment to count their individual buttons. Then one by one, record the number of buttons each child has—include those that have zero buttons. Students (or you) can then use calculators as a tool to calculate the total number of buttons for the class. Students may want to keep a button count over the course of a week or the unit! Many students like to attempt to reach 100 buttons per day. You will be amazed at the layers they wear to "up" the count!

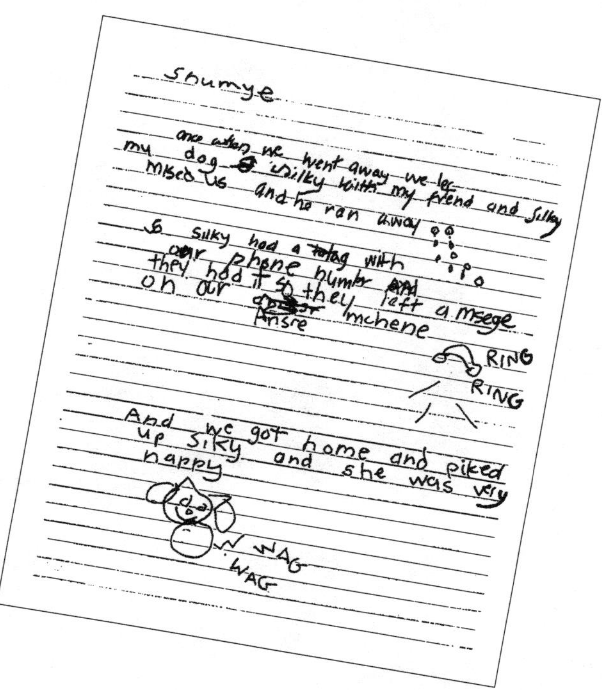

5. Just as Toad lost his button in the story, all of us have lost something. Have students think about something they have lost. How did they feel? What did they do? Did they find it? To help them get started, pair students. For one minute, have each student tell a partner about something that he lost. Then have students switch roles. Second and third grade students can write about their experience. Share stories with the group.

6. Adapt songs to relate to buttons. One teacher reported that her class sang "Did You Ever See A Button?" to the tune of "Did You Ever See A Laddie/Lassie?" to review button attributes. Many teachers have also suggested singing the "Hello My Name Is Joe" song about a worker in a button factory.

Modifications for Kindergarten

- After reading the story to the children, have them freely explore the buttons for about 10 minutes or as long as interest is sustained. Meet back in the group area. Ask what they discovered about the buttons. If they are ready to focus on attributes, play the "Button Up" game with a set of buttons that have easily identifiable attributes and allow the children to stand up many times.

- After a second session of free exploration with buttons, have each student choose a favorite button. Make a class book of students' favorite buttons. Encourage each student to draw a large picture of his or her button. Then they can dictate one or more words that describe their button's attributes for an adult to write down.

Optional: Students can trace over the written word(s).

Session 2: Sort, Classify, and "Guess the Sort"

Overview

In this session, students continue to explore button attributes as they sort their buttons in a variety of ways. They begin by helping the teacher sort a group of *felt* buttons by color. Then, they work with a partner to sort *real* buttons by color. Students try new ways to sort, first as a whole group, then independently with their partners. Finally, teams classify their buttons in any way they choose, and everyone has fun guessing how the buttons were sorted by their classmates.

One delightful way to introduce the directed sorting activity is the storybook The Button Box. *In this story a young child visits his grandmother who has a special box full of buttons. As he explores and examines the buttons, he sorts and classifies them using the attributes of color, size, materials from which the buttons are made, and the uses of buttons.*

This session can be tailored to suit your students' abilities. For example, with older or more experienced students, you may not need to model each method of sorting with the whole group before allowing them to sort their buttons independently. You may also want to challenge your students with sorting by more than one attribute or with successive sorting.

The activities in this session encourage students to: make their own discoveries in an open-ended setting; look at shapes and relationships in geometry; solve problems with concrete materials; increase observation and logical thinking skills; analyze data; work cooperatively; and connect mathematics to their everyday experience.

What You Need

For the class:

- ❒ felt board (from Session 1)
- ❒ black and white felt buttons (from Session 1)
- ❒ additional set of colored felt buttons
- ❒ 3 large yarn loops (for "Sorting By Size")
- ❒ card stock or "sentence strips"
- ❒ felt pen
- ❒ *(optional)* 8 small yarn loops (any bright color that contrasts with the color of your felt board)
- ❒ *(optional)* copy of the book, *The Button Box* by Margarette S. Reid

For each pair of students:

- ❒ 1 cup of 40–50 buttons (from Session 1)

Getting Ready

1. Cut buttons out of 9"x 12" rectangles of colored felt to make a collection of felt buttons as follows:

RED Felt Buttons
1 large, round with four holes
1 small, round with two holes
1 small, round with one hole
1 small, square with two holes

DARK BLUE Felt Buttons
1 large, round with four holes
1 large, round with two holes
1 large, triangular with three holes
1 small, square with one hole

YELLOW Felt Buttons
1 small, round with two holes
1 small, round with four holes
1 small, square with three holes

PINK Felt Buttons
1 large, square with four holes
1 small, round with one hole
1 small, round with two holes
1 small, round with four holes
1 small, triangular with one hole

BLACK Felt Buttons
1 small, round with one hole
1 small, round with three holes
1 small, square with two holes

WHITE Felt Buttons
1 small, round with one hole
1 small, round with three holes
1 small, triangular with two holes

Other colors can be substituted, with consideration given to the color of the felt board being used. **Be sure that there is color contrast so that the buttons stand out on the felt board.**

2. Make the yarn loops that you want to use. For the small loops, cut 8 one-yard pieces of yarn, then tie the ends of each piece together to make a loop. For the large loops, cut 3 two-yard pieces of yarn, then tie the ends of each piece together to make a loop.

3. Cut three 9" lengths of "sentence strips," or cut an 8 1/2" x 11" piece of card stock into three long strips. These cards will be used to record words to describe button sizes.

4. Have the following materials handy in the group area: a felt board, the set of felt buttons from Session 1 and the set of colored felt buttons made for this session, yarn loops, three cards, a felt pen; and three real buttons as follows: one small, one medium, and one large.

5. For each pair of students, fill one cup with 40–50 buttons. Distribute them as in Session 1.

Sorting, Classifying, and Guessing!

1. Gather the students on the rug or a group area away from their desks. Have the empty felt board where all children can see it.

2. Ask the students questions about "The Lost Button" story read in Session 1, such as:

> *Who were the two friends in the story?* [Frog and Toad]
>
> *What happened in the story?* [Toad lost his button.]
>
> *Did Toad's friends try to help him find his button?* [Yes]
>
> *What kind of buttons did they find?* [As the children respond here, put up the various buttons that they describe on the felt board.]
>
> *What did Toad say each time he received a button?* [That is not my button!]
>
> *Did he ever find it?* [Yes] *Where*? [On the floor in his home.]
>
> *What did it look like?* [Large, round, white, four-holed, thick button] Put Toad's button up on the felt board.

3. Tell the children that they are going to investigate a new cup of buttons with a new partner. (You may want to use random selection for pairing students.) Again, it is very important that students have additional time to explore these relatively new and attractive buttons! Allow pairs of students to go to their tables.

4. While students are engaged with the buttons, replace the felt buttons that are on the felt board with the colored felt buttons. Then circulate to observe what your students are doing with the buttons.

5. After 5–10 minutes, use a signal to get the children's attention. Invite them back to the group area, away from their desks. Ask what they have discovered about their new cup of buttons.

6. Optional: Read *The Button Box* story to springboard into the sorting activity you choose to do.

Sorting by Color

1. Show the students the felt board with the colored buttons on it. Ask the children for ways to put them in groups. Accept all ideas. Use color as the first attribute to sort the felt buttons. This attribute works well visually and is the first way most children sort. After the groups are made according to color on the felt board, you *may* choose to place one small yarn loop around each group of buttons. Have students make observations about the groups of buttons. Assist students if necessary by asking questions, such as:

> *How many buttons are yellow? black? red? pink? white?*
>
> *What color has the most buttons in the group? the fewest?*
>
> *Did any groups have the same number of buttons as another group?*

As an alternative to having children come to the group area and return to their seats for each sort, some teachers have chosen to model fewer sorts, while other teachers have taught Session 2 on two different days.

2. Tell children that they will now return to their places and sort their buttons by color. Remind them to work as partners to sort the buttons. Briefly discuss what to do if there's disagreement about colors. [They could invent a new category for "unusual colors," "multi-colored," or just "hard to classify" buttons.]

3. Have a student repeat the directions back to the class for additional clarity. You may want to direct children by the colors they are wearing, saying, for example, "Anyone who is wearing green may go to their table."

4. Circulate as the children sort their buttons. Check with pairs of students and listen to their color categories. Ask questions about the different color groups they created.

5. When they have finished sorting by color, ask each student to choose a favorite button and bring it to the group area.

Sorting by Size

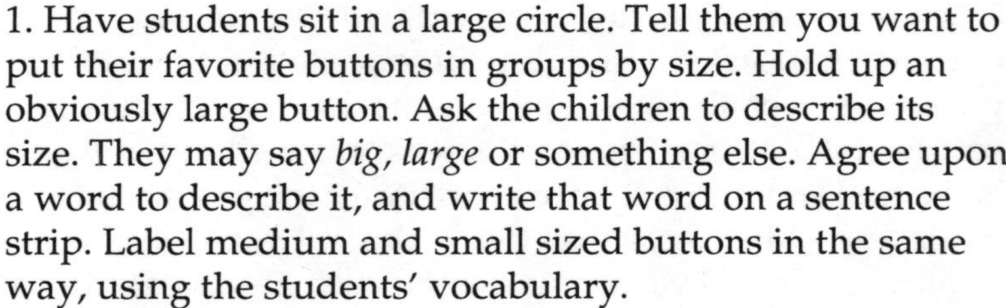

1. Have students sit in a large circle. Tell them you want to put their favorite buttons in groups by size. Hold up an obviously large button. Ask the children to describe its size. They may say *big, large* or something else. Agree upon a word to describe it, and write that word on a sentence strip. Label medium and small sized buttons in the same way, using the students' vocabulary.

2. Put the three large yarn loops on the floor in the middle of the group. Into each loop, place a word card with the sample button that corresponds to it. Ask students to predict by a show of "thumbs up" or "thumbs down" which loop will have the most buttons after everyone has placed their favorite button in a loop.

3. Ask, "Who has a small button?" Select a volunteer to put her button in a loop. Ask the class if they agree with the placement. Ask if someone has a button that can go in a different loop. Have him place his button in a loop. Engage the whole group by asking for agreement as buttons are placed in loops. Continue until about half of the buttons are in loops. Now ask students to predict which loop will have the most buttons when the sort is completed. Have the rest of the class, one by one, place their buttons into the appropriate loops. Ask a student to explain how the buttons were sorted.

4. Ask for observations about the button groupings. Count the buttons in each loop. *Which loop of buttons has the most? the fewest? Do any loops have the same number of buttons? How many buttons are there in all?*

5. Tell the children that they are going to return to their seats to sort their group of buttons by size just as their favorite buttons were sorted. Ask how many groups they will have. [Three] Ask them to identify the three groups they will make. [Large, medium, and small.] This time, you could use the length of their hair (long, medium, and short) as the attribute to send children back to their tables. Have children take their favorite button back to their work areas.

6. Circulate around the room. After you observe that most children have completed the task, have the children "freeze." Ask how they sorted their buttons. [Size]

7. Ask for partners to report about the groups they created. Help with questions such as, *What size button did you have the most of? the fewest? Did any groups of buttons have the same number?*

Inventing New Ways to Sort

1. Ask the children to return again to the group area. Hold up the felt board that has the color sort still on it. Ask how those buttons were sorted. [Color] Remove the loops. Ask students for another way to sort the buttons. Take all suggestions.

2. Try out a new sort, such as the number of holes each button has. After sorting the felt buttons, put loops around each group. Count the buttons in each loop. Make comparisons about the groups. Take the loops off again.

3. Sort with another attribute, such as shape. Loop the groups. Count buttons in each loop. Compare the number of buttons in each loop.

4. Have partners return to their buttons. This time, give students the opportunity to sort the buttons any way(s) they choose.

5. After 5 minutes, have students stop working and leave their buttons sorted on the table.

Encourage students to play this game very quietly with their partners, so everyone else has a chance to guess the sort too.

6. With their partners, have students walk around the room and look at the ways that the buttons were sorted by their classmates. Students can now play "Guess the Sort." Can they guess the way in which the buttons were sorted at each work space?

Going Further

1. Shoe Sort. Have each student take off one shoe and place it in the center of the circle. Brainstorm the attributes of the shoes. [Tie, velcro, slip-on, colors, sizes, high-tops, tennis shoes, dress-up, etc.] Sort the shoes several times using different attributes. Choose one (or more) of these wonderful books to accompany this activity: *Alligator Shoes* by Arthur Dorros, *Shoes* by Elizabeth Winthrop, and *Whose Shoes Are These?* by Ron Roy.

2. "People Sorting" Game. Have students sit in a circle in the group area. Choose an attribute to sort out a group of students. Start with an easily visible trait, such as hair color. Do not reveal the trait to the class. Call students, one at a time, into the center of the circle until there are three students in the circle. Tell the class these students have something in common. Can they guess what it is? Call another two students into the circle. Ask if there are any students who think they can join the group in the center. Continue until they have figured out the sort. Play this game at various times. Use many physical traits and, in addition, include attributes related to students' clothing such as long sleeves, stripes, dresses, blue jeans, and colors.

3. Classroom Collections of Materials. Have the class make collections of other small items that can be sorted. Children can bring some items from home and/or the class can go on scavenger hunts to acquire materials. Some items that can be gathered are: rocks, shells, acorns, seeds, bottle caps, keys, etc. There is a letter to parents on page 70 to assist you with this project.

4. Buttons from Home. For homework, have students select a button from home. Record all the attributes of the button. Draw a button that has only one of the same attributes as the selected button and record the attributes that are different.

5. Button Trains. Have students make trains of buttons.

a. Pattern Trains: Students use buttons to make a long train (line) of buttons that follow a pattern. Some examples include lining up buttons by: color (black, red, red, black, red, red...); size (small, medium, large, small, medium, large...); number of holes (2 holes, 2 holes, shank, 4 holes, 2 holes, 2 holes, shank, 4 holes...); and other variations on patterns that students create.

b. Attribute Trains: The object is to make a long train (line) of buttons so that the buttons next to each other have an attribute in common. Have each student select one button. Start by putting one button down. Observe that button's attributes—large, shank, shell, shiny, smooth, etc. A person who has a button with one of those attributes states the attribute she is matching and places her button next to the first button. The new button is likely to have new and different attributes. Other students continue to place their buttons, one at a time, matching one attribute of the last button placed. To make this more challenging, increase the number of attributes that need to be matched to two or three.

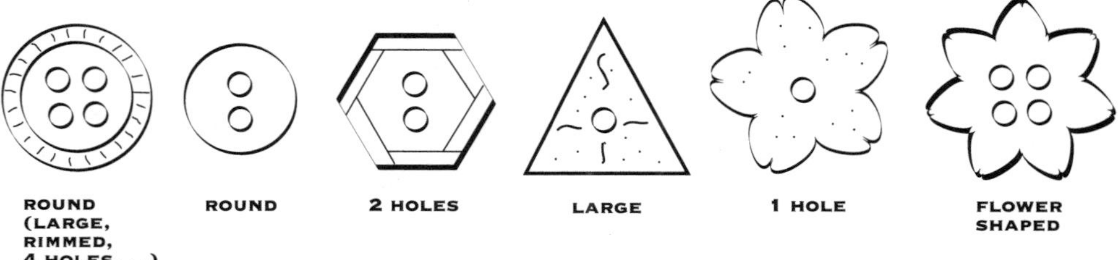

6. Successive Sorting Activity (grades 2 and 3). Model sorting buttons into two distinct groups such as: shiny/dull (not shiny); thick/thin; four-holed/not four-holed; plastic/not plastic. Encourage students to come up with as many ways as possible to sort in this fashion.

a. Put a large handful of buttons on a sheet of paper. Draw a circle around that group of buttons.

b. Ask students for one way to sort the buttons into two groups. Sort the buttons as the students suggest. There will be two groups of buttons. Draw circles around these new groups and label them.

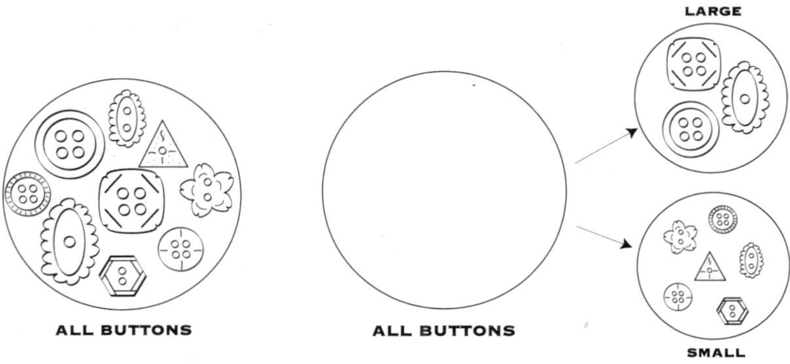

c. Now ask the students for another way to sort these two groups of buttons. How many groups will they create? [4]

d. Sort each group of buttons into two new groups according to the attribute given. Now there are eight possible groups of buttons. Draw circles around these new groups and label. There may be one or more groups without any buttons (an empty set).

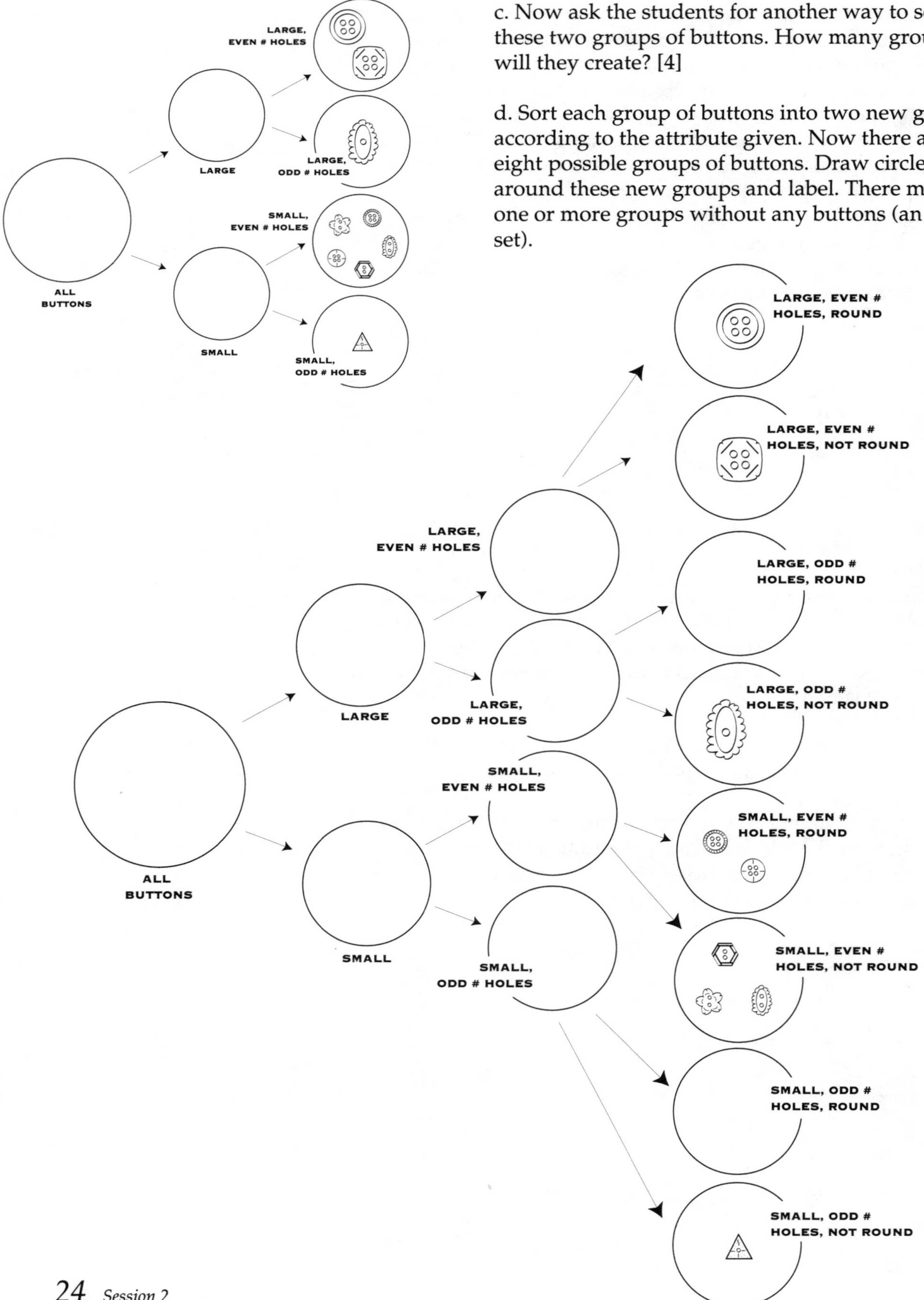

e. Ask if there is another way that the buttons can be sorted. How many groups will be formed? Are there buttons for each group?

f. Sort each pile of buttons again according to that attribute. Now there are 16 possible groups of buttons. Depending upon your attributes and number of buttons, you may have more empty groups. Label all groups.

Have students work in pairs and make their own successive sorts of buttons.

Modifications for Kindergarten

Gather the children in the group area away from tables. Begin the lesson with a review of the story, "The Lost Button" and a description of Toad's lost button. Use the felt buttons as described in the "GO" section #2 on page 18. Then send students to tables to freely explore a new cup of the buttons with a partner. Give them at least ten minutes to do this. While they are exploring, replace the felt buttons from the story with the set of colored felt buttons made in the "Getting Ready" section of this session. Circulate and observe what the children are doing with the buttons.

Have children return to the group area and report their discoveries. Sort the felt buttons with the class by color. Send the children back to their tables to sort their buttons by color. Walk around and check that partners are on task. Allow time for more play with the buttons.

Another day, begin with the felt board and assorted colored felt buttons. Sort the buttons by size—large and small. Have children go to workplaces and sort their pile into two groups—large and small. Model another way to sort the felt buttons and then have the children sort the real buttons.

Ring Toss
UNITED STATES
Perfection
Checkers
Clue
PERATION
SORRY!

Session 3: Designer Buttons

Overview

In this session, students use their imaginations to create and decorate paper buttons of many shapes and sizes. They particularly enjoy making the holes in their buttons! Be sure to see the note on page 29 about the hole-punching. These unique buttons are then sorted, classified and organized on a class graphing grid.

The activities in "Designer Buttons" are designed to encourage students to: connect art and mathematics; develop a variety of sorting methods; collect and analyze data; use geometric vocabulary in a concrete situation; strengthen their own sense of number; and generate graphs from their own world.

What You Need

For the class:

❐ graphing grid
❐ about 50 sheets of white 8 1/2" x 11" card stock, enough to make twenty 4" x 5" graph labels, plus one sheet for each student's Button Template.
❐ 1 roll of masking tape
❐ *(optional)* large "post-its" (instead of card stock graph labels)

For each group of 4–6 students:

❐ crayons or colored pens
❐ scissors
❐ pencils for writing names
❐ hole puncher(s)

For each student:

❐ 1 copy of Button Template (master included, page 32)
A Button Template for Kindergarten is on page 33

Getting Ready

1. Make a graphing grid to use with the whole class. Essentially, this is a large sheet of paper on which you have drawn intersecting lines to make boxes. Since the students will be placing their paper buttons on the grid, each "box" needs to be at least big enough to comfortably contain one large paper button (about 4"x 4"). In addition, there needs to be one column of larger boxes (6" x 4") to be used to label the columns.

a. Cut a 70" long sheet of paper from a roll of white butcher paper. Cut the width to 24".

b. On both 24" sides of the paper, measure to the mid-point (12") and make a mark. Draw a line the length of the paper, connecting the two marks.

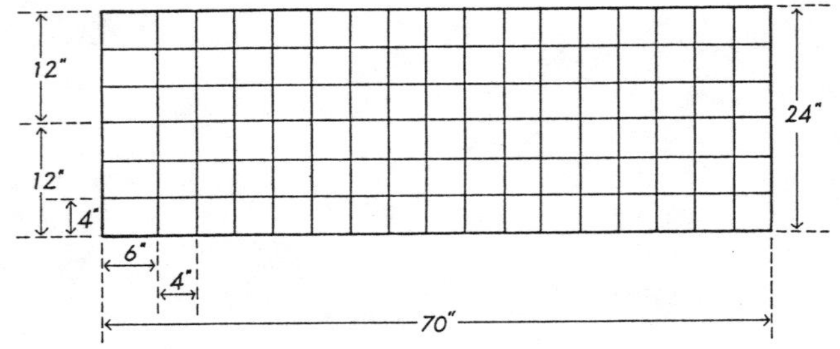

c. On both sides of that central line, draw two lines parallel to it, 4 inches apart. There are now a total of five lines running the length of the paper.

d. Next, draw vertical lines extending the width of the paper (24") to make the boxes on the grid. Starting from the left, measure six inches and make a vertical line. From this point on, measure and make a line every four inches. The finished grid will have one column of boxes 6" x 4" and 16 columns of boxes that are 4" x 4". It is advisable to laminate the grid or cover it with contact paper for greater durability.

2. Make labels for the graph. Cut card stock into twenty 4"x 5" cards that will fit at the tops of the columns of the grid. Make two sets of labels as follows: by number of holes (one hole, two holes, three holes, four holes) and by shape (circle, oval, square, triangle). On each label, draw a picture to go with the word. Keep the remaining 12 blank labels and a felt pen nearby so that you can create more labels as you graph with the students. (Large "post-its" could also be used for labels.)

3. Duplicate one copy of the Button Template master sheet (page 32) onto white card stock for each student in the class.

4. In students' work areas, place materials for the students to decorate their buttons, such as crayons, markers, colored pencils, pens, scissors and hole punchers. One hole puncher per four students works well.

5. Use masking tape to hang the graph on the chalkboard, bulletin board or wall in the area where you will gather the class after they make their buttons. If you hang the graph so it stretches horizontally, it fits better and is easier to see. Make one small masking tape loop (sticky side out) for each child to use to attach his button to the graph. Make six extra loops for the graph's label cards. Stick the tape loops to a nearby surface, so they'll be handy for you to use.

Designing Buttons

1. Gather children in the group area. Tell them that they are going to be button designers. Show them a copy of the Button Template sheet. Have them name the shapes of the buttons. [Triangle, oval, square, circle]

2. Tell students that they will each receive a Button Template sheet. They will choose a button shape to decorate. After the button is decorated and cut out, they will punch one, two, three or four holes in the button. Explain that if there is extra time, they can continue to decorate other buttons on their sheets.

*Children love to punch holes! To get some of the hole-punching out of their systems, it is helpful to make the hole punchers available for free exploration for a few days before this activity. This way you may avoid having a set of **all** four-holed buttons for the graph!*

3. Have students go to work stations and complete as many buttons as they can in 15–20 minutes. Circulate and help students punch holes in their buttons as needed. Encourage students to make their own unique buttons.

4. When everyone has completed at least one button, signal for attention. Ask the students to choose **one** favorite button and write their names or initials on the back. Have students clean up scraps. Collect scissors, hole punchers, and writing implements. Decide whether you want to have the students bring their favorite buttons to the group area, or remain in their seats.

Your students may want more time to decorate the buttons. This activity could be sent home for homework or done during another class period.

5. Focus the children's attention on the graphing grid. Ask for their observations. Hold up the card labeled "one hole," and ask a volunteer to read it. Attach it to the graph with a masking tape loop in the top box of the first column on the left of the grid. Continue in this way, labeling the four long rows. Read the four cards from top to bottom.

1 HOLE						
2 HOLES						
3 HOLES						
4 HOLES						

6. Tell the children that they are going to graph the buttons that they made according to the number of holes in the button. Ask for a volunteer to place her button on the graphing grid. After it is placed check to see if the class agrees with her placement. Why do they agree or disagree?

7. Choose another volunteer. Have that student put his button on the graph. Ask if there is someone who has a button that can be placed in a different row than the other two buttons. Have her put the button in the appropriate place. Do other students agree? Disagree? Why?

8. Continue until approximately half of the students have placed their buttons on the graphing grid. Ask for predictions about which row will have the most buttons and the fewest buttons.

9. Have each student place a button on the graph. When the process is complete, look at the graph and ask for observations about it.

10. To guide your students' observations, ask number and comparison questions, such as:

How many buttons have three holes?

Did more students make buttons with one hole or two holes?

How many more buttons have __hole(s) than __holes?

Do fewer buttons have four holes or two holes? How many fewer?

If the one-holed and three-holed buttons are put together, how many buttons would there be?

How many buttons are there all together on the graph?

11. Take the "number of holes" label cards off the graph.
Have students remove their buttons from the grid, row by row.

12. Take out the the cards labeled with the shapes. You may have to make an additional card with a shape that a student created, i.e., a rectangle. As before, label the rows with the shape cards.

13. Ask children to predict how the graph will look when the buttons are graphed by shape. Which shape will have the most buttons in its row? the fewest? Have children place their buttons on the graph. Complete the graph and have the students make observations.

14. Depending on student interest, you may want to have students remove their buttons again. Brainstorm other ways to graph the buttons. Decide upon one way and make labels for it. Have students graph the buttons and make observations.

Going Further

1. Real World Connection:

a. Working in partners, have students take a handful of real buttons and graph them according to the number of holes. Ask students what the most common number of holes is. Why do they think that is? What would be taken into consideration when making holes in buttons? Combine the information from all the graphs created by student pairs and determine the totals for the number of buttons with one hole, two holes, three holes, etc. Are the results of the whole group similar to the results of their individual graphs?

b. Next, have students look at the buttons on their clothing. What is the most common number of holes in their buttons? How do the results generated by buttons on their clothing compare to the graph created from handfuls of buttons?

c. Have students investigate the number of holes in the buttons on their families' clothing that evening. Report their results and combine the data. Compare the data gathered in class to the data generated from home. Can students come to any conclusion about the most common number of holes in a button? What other type of research might they do to further investigate the most common number of holes in a button?

2. Just as Toad sewed buttons on his jacket, the children can glue one of their buttons onto a large paper "jacket."

3. Make "real graphs" by using collections of things in the classroom to make the graphs, such as plastic animals, shells, rocks, or bottle caps.

4. For homework, students can graph something in the home, such as shoes, silverware, writing implements, toys, or cans of food.

5. Have each student bring a stuffed animal from home. Brainstorm ways to graph the animals. As a class, sort and graph the animals in a variety of ways.

As a follow-up on shapes, read The Secret Birthday Message *by Eric Carle. In this story, Tim gets a mysterious letter the night before his birthday written in a code using shapes. Children fully participate in this enticing adventure as they turn each full-color page, designed with cut-out shapes. Children can then design a shape book of their own!*

Modifications for Kindergarten

Use the button template with only four large buttons. Give children an opportunity to look at each other's buttons before doing the graphing activity. Do only one graph the first time with the children, using **shape** as the attribute to classify.

Have students bring something from home that can fit in their hand *and* has the shape of a square, circle, oval, or triangle. Have students share their items at group time. Graph the items by shape. Ask children for other ways to graph the items. Graph them in these ways.

Button Template

Kindergarten Button Template

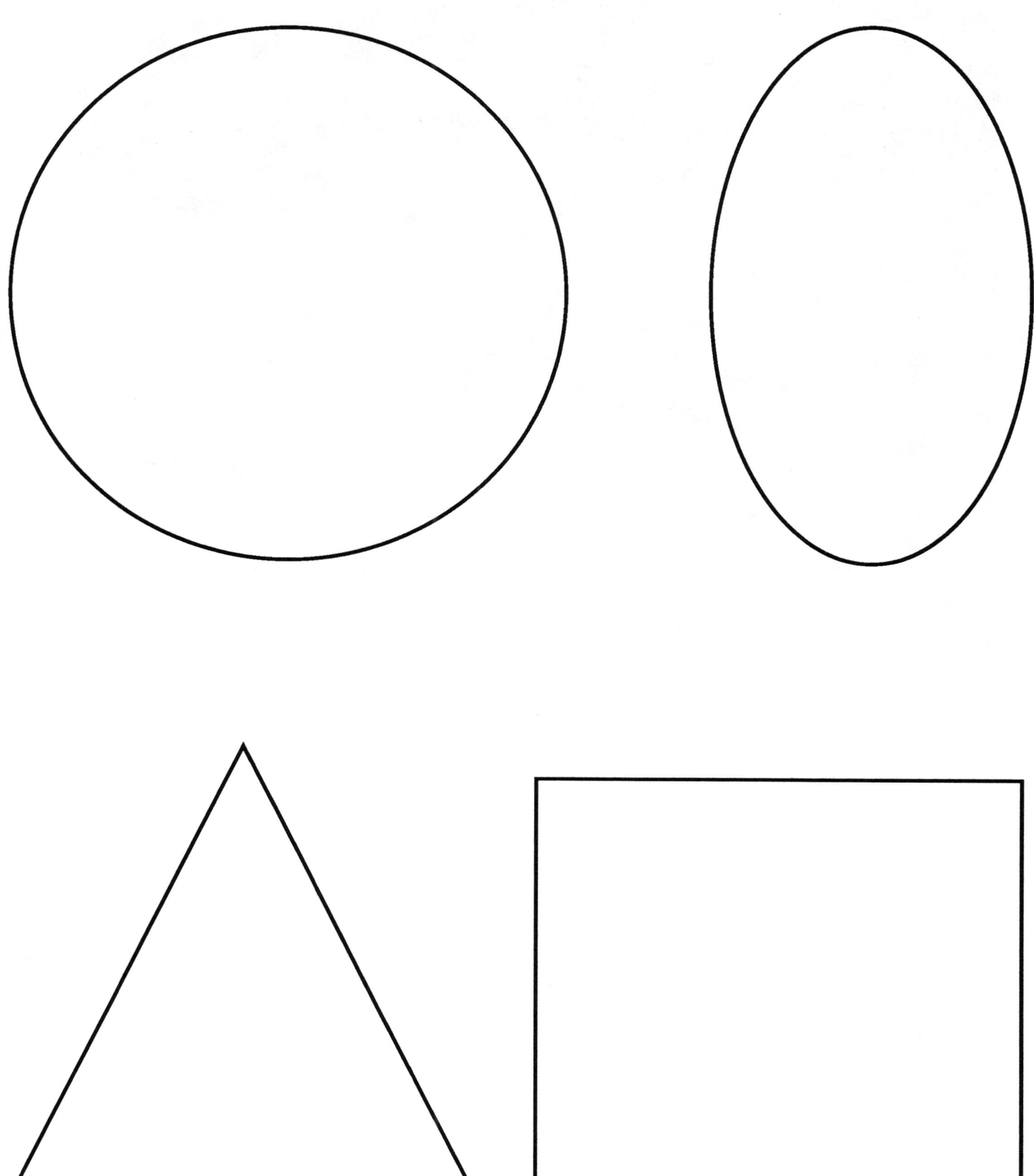

ones
tens

Session 4: Frog Guesstimation

Overview

In this activity, children use a jar full of frogs to begin an exploration of estimation—affectionately referred to as "guesstimation" by young students. The teacher records the group's first estimates in a non-competitive way. As the frogs are poured out and counted on a place value board, the children have several opportunities to revise their estimates. Students in first grade and above who are developmentally ready can then work individually to estimate and count a handful of lima beans on their own place value boards. Teachers of younger students may want to skip the lima bean estimation. Please note that "Modifications for Kindergarten" for this session are suggested on page 43.

It is important for your students to know that estimation is not a contest! You can foster a non-competitive atmosphere by stressing that there are no winner or losers. Validate all estimates by saying that there are some "closer" estimates but no "wrong" estimates. Let students know that with practice, they will all become more skillful at making estimates.

Estimation is an essential life skill. People make estimates every day, such as what the grocery bill will add up to at the check-out counter or how many baskets of strawberries are needed for eight people. When children are given opportunities to make estimates, they increase their understanding of computation, numbers, and quantities, while gaining an enhanced sense of what a reasonable range of possible answers to problems might be, not only in mathematics and science, but also in many other aspects of life and work.

The activities in this session encourage your students to: use concrete materials for estimation; develop the courage and confidence to make a guess and to revise it as more information is revealed; strengthen their understanding of place value; generate and organize data.

What You Need

For the class:

- ❒ a small plastic jar
- ❒ 27–99 small plastic frogs (several sources from which to order these are listed on page 71)
- ❒ large place value counting board (see "Getting Ready," #2 for how to make this board from the master on pages 92–93)
- ❒ 2–7 clear plastic cups (for teacher to use to count frogs with the large place value board)
- ❒ 1 pad of 3" square "post-its"
- ❒ dark felt markers
- ❒ 3 pounds of large lima beans
- ❒ 4 large ziplock bags

For each student:

- ❒ card stock place value board (see "Getting Ready," #3 for how to make these boards from master on page 44)
- ❒ 8 small paper cups (for student to use to count beans with the small place value boards)
- ❒ large lima beans (a handful from the bag above)
- ❒ 1 small empty container, 8 ounce size (to carry the handful of beans back to seat)

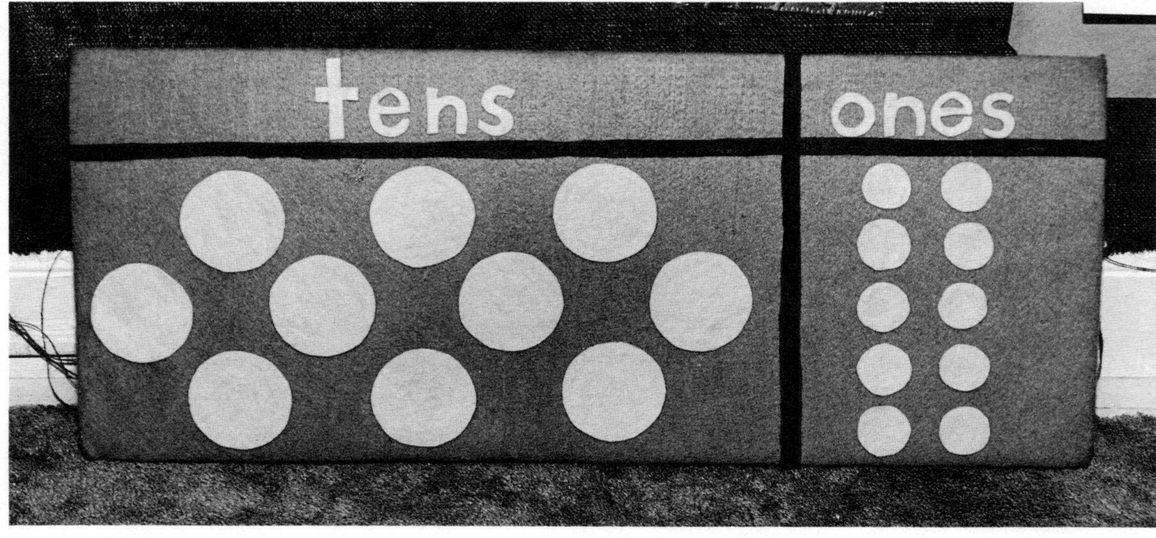

Getting Ready

1. Fill a small plastic jar with a number of small plastic frogs. For kindergarten, put 36 frogs in the jar; for first grade, put 48 frogs in the jar; for second grade, 57 frogs, and for third grade, 68 frogs. Based on the experience and abilities of your students, you may need to lower or raise the number of frogs for the estimation. Be sure that the number of frogs is no greater than 99 or no less than 27 so that students can gain an understanding of the place value board as a tool for counting.

2. Duplicate one large place value board (pages 92–93). Use rubber cement to glue the board onto a sheet of tagboard or matté board. You may wish to laminate the board or cover it with clear contact paper for greater durability. *Note:* Some teachers have enlarged the board for greater visibility while other teachers have used felt to make the board.

3. Duplicate one copy of the student place value board (page 44) onto standard (8 1/2" x 11") colored card stock paper (or construction paper) for each student in the class.

4. Divide the three pounds of *large* lima beans equally into two–four large ziplock bags, depending upon the number of stations you want to set up for students to take handfuls of beans.

Some teachers have painted lima beans green to better represent frogs.

5. **Before the day of the activity**, show the jar of frogs to your students. Invite them to take a careful look at the frogs in the jar. However, do not let them open the jar.

6. On the **day of** the presentation:

a. Gather the large place value board and small plastic cups as follows: four cups for first grade; five for second grade; and six for third grade. (The number of cups is the same as the tens' digit in the number of frogs that you use.)

b. Have a copy of the student place value board; ten paper cups; two–four large ziplock bags filled with the lima beans; and one pad of 3" square "post-its" at the group area.

c. Place at each student's desk or work space (or have ready for quick distribution): a student place value board, eight paper cups, a dark felt marker, and a "post-it" to record the estimate.

Part 1: Guesstimating Frogs

1. Gather students in a circle in an area away from their desks. Hold up the small jar filled with plastic frogs. Tell the class that they are going to guess (estimate) how many frogs are in the jar. Ask for volunteers to make guesses.

Many teachers found that their students stayed more engaged in this part of the activity when the students wrote the number in the air with their finger while they recorded the number on the board.

2. As each student gives an estimate, ask the student to tell you how to write the number. As you record it on the chalkboard, students can use their index finger to write the number in the air. If a student gives an estimate that has already been recorded, underline the original estimate. However, if you begin to get a large number of students giving the same estimate, acknowledge the estimate. Then ask the class for any other *new* estimates. **Keep estimates anonymous so when you refer back to them at the end, students will not evaluate each other's estimates.**

3. After all the estimates are recorded, ask students for the highest (largest) and lowest (smallest) estimates. Circle those two estimates. Explain that this represents the ***range*** of estimates that were made by the class. Ask if they think the actual number of frogs will be between those two numbers.

4. Ask the students how to determine the actual number of frogs. [Count them!]

5. Show the students the place value counting board. Ask for observations about the board. Point out the two sides: tens' side and ones' side. Count the number of circles on each side. Tell the students that they will be using the board to help count the frogs.

*You may need to remind the class more than once that this is not a contest or a "winning" game! This is guesstimating! There are some "closer" answers, but **no** "wrong" answers. Keep estimations anonymous; there is no need to write names next to guesses.*

6. Open the jar and pour out the frogs. Now that they see the frogs out of the jar, have the children look at the frogs again. Ask if anyone would like to change his estimate. Listen to some of the new estimates. This time the estimates will only be recorded mentally, not written on the board. Ask, by a show of hands, how many students would make a higher (larger) estimate? A lower (smaller) estimate? How many would keep their original estimate?

7. Using the place value board, begin counting the frogs. Have the students count with you as each frog is placed on a circle on the ones' side. When the ones' side is filled with ten frogs, model how the place value board works. Make a group of ten frogs, put the ten frogs in a clear plastic cup, and place it on the tens' side.

8. Ask how many frogs are on the board. [Ten] Continue by counting frogs on the one's side, one by one, until the one's side has ten more frogs on it. Ask the students what to do with the group of ten frogs on the ones' side. [Make a group of ten, put the ten frogs in a cup and place it on the tens' side.] Ask how many frogs are now on the board? [Twenty]

You may want to have students record their frog estimates on a paper strip. As frogs are counted out, give students several opportunities to adjust their estimates. Each new estimate should be written directly below the previous one on the paper strip. Lastly, students should also record on the strip the actual number of frogs. The students' records can be used to assess their individual estimation process.

9. Point out the number of frogs on the board and the number of frogs that have not been counted. Ask students if they want to change their estimates. Have them make new mental estimates if they choose.

10. Continue counting frogs, stopping to ask students what to do whenever you have ten frogs on the ones' side. Stop occasionally to ask, "How many frogs are on the board?" Count the cups by tens as a group, "Ten, twenty, thirty."

11. Have students make one more mental estimate when the pile of uncounted frogs has dwindled to a dozen or so. Ask questions such as, "How many of you think we will get to a hundred? How many think we will get to seventy-five?"

12. Finish counting the frogs. There will be fewer than ten on the ones' side. Ask students why you cannot put those frogs in a cup. Ask how many frogs are in the jar. Review the number of tens and ones. [How many cups? How many frogs left on the one's side?]

13. Ask students how to record the actual number of frogs. Then record the number on the board.

14. Compare the actual number of frogs to the recorded estimates. With student input, draw a line through the estimates that are clearly too large or too small. Find the estimate(s) that is(are) closest to the actual. How far from the actual number was that estimate? Again, if necessary, remind students that this is not a contest or win/lose game.

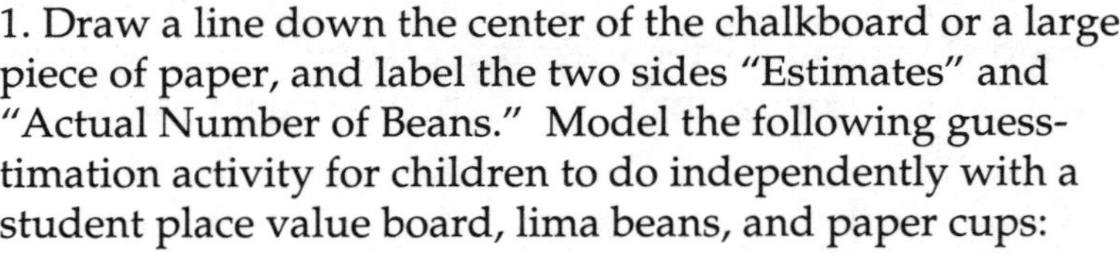

Part 2: Guesstimating Handfuls of Lima Beans (Grades 1–3)

If this activity is not appropriate for your students, end the session with Part 1.

1. Draw a line down the center of the chalkboard or a large piece of paper, and label the two sides "Estimates" and "Actual Number of Beans." Model the following guesstimation activity for children to do independently with a student place value board, lima beans, and paper cups:

> a. Tell the children that they are going to go to one of four bags of beans to get a handful of lima beans. Define a "handful" of beans as the amount of beans that fit comfortably in a closed hand. Demonstrate how to take a handful of lima beans. Put your hand in the lima bean bag and grab some beans. Shake your hand so that any excess beans will fall. Turn your hand upside-down to see if any more beans fall out. The beans that remain in your hand are a "handful" of beans. For extra emphasis, you could also model the "wrong" way to get a handful of beans, by using two hands, grabbing too many and dropping some on the floor.

> b. Empty the handful into a small container. Make a guess as to the number of beans in that handful. Write the estimate on the chalkboard on the side labeled, "Estimates."
>
> c. Model counting the beans using a student place value board and paper cups in the same manner as you counted the frogs.
>
> d. Record the actual number of beans with a dark marker on a "post-it" and put it on the other side of the chalkboard, labeled, "Actual Number of Beans."

2. Explain that four students at a time will go to the four ziplock bags. Each student will take a handful of beans and empty it into a container. Remind students to make estimates and to record their estimates on the chalkboard under the heading "Estimates."

3. Let the students begin. As they begin to use a place value board to count the beans, walk around and give each student a "post-it" to record the actual number.

4. As students finish counting the beans, have them record the actual number on the "post-it" that you left at their desks and put it up on the side of the chalkboard labeled, "Actual Number of Beans."

If your students are having trouble organizing the data, you may want to suggest that they use a number line. The data can be organized in the form of a bar graph or clustered by groups of tens, such as 10s, 20s, 30s, and so on.

5. When all students have posted their results, collect the containers of beans. Focus attention on the range under "Estimates" and circle the highest and lowest in each category. Then look at the numbers under the "Actual Number of Beans" and again circle the highest and lowest numbers. Make comparisons about these ranges.

6. Focus the students' attention on the the data for the actual number of beans in a handful. Ask how the data could be organized so it is easy to read and interpret. Try arranging the "post-its" **more than one way**—according to student suggestions. Make observations each time the data is organized. For example, ask what the most common number of beans in a handful was? Look for other patterns in the data. Discuss the data for as long as time and interest allow.

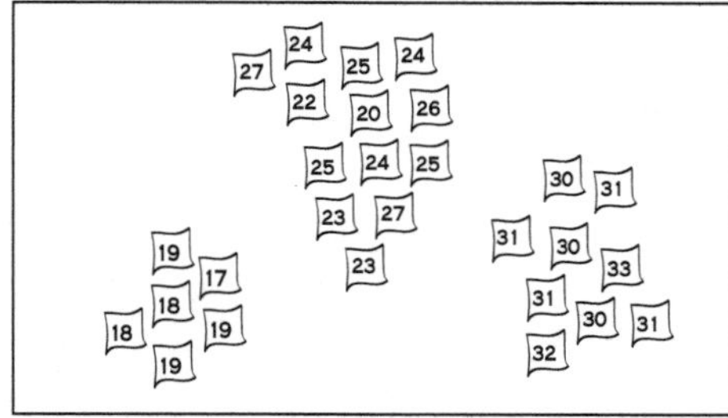
CLUSTERING DATA

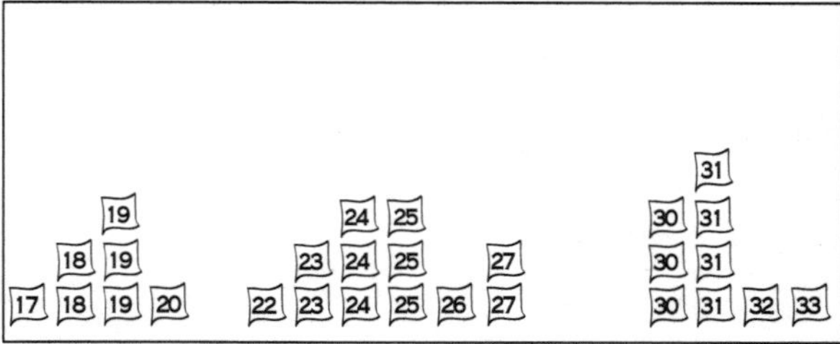
BAR GRAPH

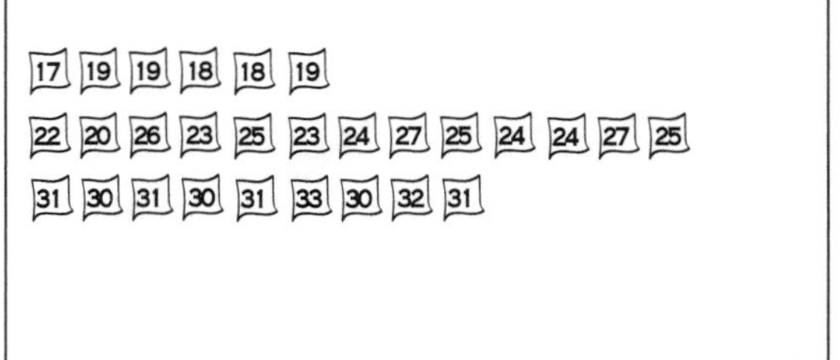

ORGANIZING BY 10'S

Going Further

One way to incorporate at least one estimation problem into each week's curriculum is to have an Estimation (or Guesstimation) Station on a bulletin board. (In classrooms where calendar activities are done, this Estimation Station can be included in the weekly activities.) The type of estimate can vary. Begin with a small number of common items such as 36 bottle caps. On Monday, put the caps in a clear plastic bag. Staple the bag on the board, and post a sheet with the question, "How many bottle caps are in the bag?" Point out the estimation problem at calendar time. During the week, students can record their guesstimates on the sheet. For example, it could look like this:

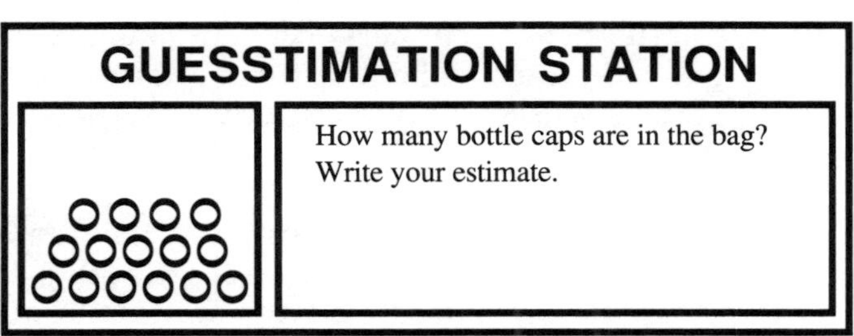

On Friday, estimation becomes the focus for a lesson in counting and place value. Gather students in an area away from their desks. To begin, have your students look at their recorded estimates made during the week. Ask which number is the highest estimate and which is the lowest. Then pour the bottle caps out. The students may want to make another *mental* estimate after seeing the bottle caps spread out. Use the place value board in the same way it was used for the frog and bean estimates to determine the actual number. Record the actual number on the sheet where the students' estimates were written. Make comparisons between the estimates and the actual numbers.

Limiting Variables in Estimations

To help students develop their estimation skills, keep one variable the same when creating a new estimation. Then students can apply prior knowledge to a new estimation. For example, after doing the frog estimation in one size jar, use either a larger or smaller jar and fill that jar with the frogs. Students will have a point of reference from which they can make their estimation. This also provides an informal assessment for you. If students do not adjust their estimate according to the known information from the initial frog estimation, they are likely to need more practice with numbers and gaining number sense.

The other variable that can be held constant is the container. Then significantly change the size of the objects to estimate and observe how your students adjust their estimations.

Challenging Estimations

- Using footsteps as a measure, estimate the number of steps: from one wall in the classroom to the opposite wall; from the classroom door to the restroom; from the classroom door to the office; and from the classroom to the yard.

- Using popcorn as a measure, estimate the number of small paper cupfuls of popcorn that: one quarter of a cup of kernels will make; one half of a cup of kernels will make; three quarters of a cup of kernels will make; and one cup of kernels will make.

- Using measures of rice, estimate the number of: cups of rice that will fit into a large bottle; half cups of rice that will fit into a large bottle; and quarter cups of rice that will fit into a large bottle.

Suggestions for Grade 3

Fill 2–4 bags of the same size with similar items like pinto, lima, red, or black beans. Have students work in groups and investigate questions such as: *How many beans are in each? What are some ways to determine the number of beans other than counting every bean in each of the bags?*

Modifications for Kindergarten

At the kindergarten level, use only 36 frogs in Part 1: "Frog Guesstimation." (If you do this activity early in the year or your students have not had much experience with numbers, you may want to use as few as 27 frogs.) Expect some unusual estimates, such as a low of 5 or a high of 100. Children who have difficulty making their own guesses may choose to agree with a guess that was already made. In time and with practice, all students can make guesses on their own. End this lesson after the frogs are counted out on the place value board. Omit the lima bean estimation.

Continue doing similar estimation problems with the whole group. Use a small jar full of high interest items such as plastic dinosaurs, stickers, marbles, or shells. Have the jar available for students to view the day before the estimation.

tens	ones

tens	ones

Session 5: The Frog Pond Game

Overview

In this game, pairs of students try to catch a "Magic" Frog, the last of ten frogs in a pond. Catching frogs is fun, but there's lots more to the game than that!

The Frog Pond game is an adaptation of the ancient Chinese logic game known as NIM. Like NIM, Frog Pond requires players to develop and refine logical thinking skills as they experiment with different strategies. When students have mastered the game, teachers can change the rules to make the last frog a "Poison" Frog. The students' strategies will change, too!

Playing the Frog Pond game encourages your students to: use concrete materials to play a game cooperatively; strengthen logical thinking skills; look for patterns related to the quantity of ten; develop, verbalize (or write), test, and refine strategies.

Throughout this session, avoid telling your students how to catch the magic frog! Their thinking strategies are best developed through experimentation. In addition, observing your students' strategy development will help you informally assess their thinking and problem-solving skills.

What You Need

For the class:

- ❒ large Frog Pond gameboard (master on pages 94–95)
- ❒ 10 large plastic frogs (or buttons, bottle caps, beans, etc.)
- ❒ 1 green felt marker or crayon
- ❒ 1 blue felt marker or crayon
- ❒ 12" x 18" piece of green tagboard or matté board
- ❒ rubber cement
- ❒ 18 sheets of standard (8 1/2" x 11") paper to duplicate student gameboards, preferably in blue

Optional: To make the extra-large Frog Pond gameboard:

- ❒ 26" x 18" piece of green tagboard or matté board
- ❒ 24" x 16" sheet of blue construction paper or blue fadeless paper
- ❒ 10 paper frogs (duplicated from page 52)
- ❒ (*optional*) laminator or clear contact paper

For each pair of students:

- ❒ small Frog Pond gameboard (master on page 53)
- ❒ 10 small plastic frogs (or buttons, bottle caps, beans, etc.)
- ❒ small paper cups (same as those used in Session 4)

Getting Ready

1. Color in the frogs with a green marker and the water with a blue marker on the 11" x 17" Frog Pond gameboard. Cut around the edge of the pond. Use rubber cement to attach it to a 12" x 18" piece of green tagboard. Laminate or cover with contact paper. For greater visibility while modeling, some teachers have found it helpful to use a larger size board. You can make a 26" x 18" larger gameboard as follows:

    a. Make two copies of the sheet with large frogs on page 52 so that you will have a total of 10 large paper frogs. Duplicate on green paper or color the frogs green.

    b. Cut a "pond" shape out of a 24" x 16" sheet of blue construction paper or blue fadeless paper. Make the pond large enough so that it covers most of the piece of green tagboard. Use rubber cement to attach it to a 26" x 18" green tagboard. If only white tagboard is available, color the area that surrounds the pond green.

    c. Glue the 10 green paper frogs onto the "pond" so that the frogs are situated in a similar way to the frogs on the student gameboard.

    d. Laminate or cover with contact paper.

2. Purchase 10 large frogs that are approximately the same size as the frogs on the gameboard from a local store or from a source listed on page 72.

3. Duplicate the student-size gameboards on card stock or construction paper (preferably blue) so that each pair of students has one board.

One teacher used green unifix cubes to represent the frogs.

4. For each pair of students, fill a small paper cup with ten small plastic frogs (or any other type of marker that will fit on the frogs drawn on the board). Place one cup of frogs and a gameboard for each pair of students in work spaces. (Or have filled cups and boards ready to distribute after modeling the game.)

5. Just before you present the game, gather the large gameboard, 10 large frogs, the student gameboards and cups of frogs (or markers) in the group area.

Playing Frog Pond

1. Gather students in an area away from their desks where all your students will be able to see the gameboard. Tell them that you have a new game to teach them called Frog Pond. Show them the gameboard. Ask how many frogs are on the board. [Ten] Count the frogs. Place the ten large frogs on the gameboard.

2. Explain how the game is played:

- Two people play the game at a time.
- They are both frog catchers.
- Each player may catch either 1 or 2 frogs at a time.
- As long as there are still frogs in the pond, players must catch frogs.
- The last frog is the "magic" frog. It is the one you *want* to catch. Please note that the "magic" frog may be caught by itself as the last frog on the board *or* it may be caught as *one of the last two* frogs on the board.

It may be helpful for students, especially first graders, to be able to see the magic frog clearly, as distinct from the other frogs. To do this, put a mark on one of the large frogs that is used to model the game.

3. Ask for a volunteer to play the game with you. Ask the volunteer if she wants to go first or second in the game. Before the first player takes any frogs, ask the class how many frogs that person can take. [One or two.] Play the game until one player has taken the last frog. The person who did *not* catch the magic frog chooses whether he will go first or second. Play another full game with the *same* student. (This models how the children will play with a partner.)

4. Show the class the student-size Frog Pond gameboard and frogs (or markers). Compare it with the large gameboard. Count the frogs on the small board. Show the students how to set up their gameboards.

5. Tell students that they will play the game with a partner. Ask for a volunteer to explain again how the game is played. Send the children to work spaces that are already set up, or distribute the gameboards, each with a cup of markers.

You may want to introduce the word "strategy" to children who do not know it—it is a very important and useful word in many contexts. Alternately, you could use other words to describe its meaning, such as a "plan" or "way" of taking the last frog or winning the game. You could ask, "Did anyone figure out a way to be sure that you would always take the last frog?"

6. After ten to fifteen minutes of play, use a signal to get the students' attention and announce that they should finish up the game they are playing and then stop. Regain their attention and ask, by a show of hands, how many students have won a game. Ask if anyone has a strategy (plan) to catch the magic frog. Listen to their ideas. List the strategies on a large sheet of butcher paper. Mention to the class that they may want to try out some of the strategies. Have students go back to their games. (*Note*: You may want to have students switch partners at this time.)

Of course, the strategies your students share at this point may be incomplete and less sophisticated than adults might mention. For example, one student may say that his strategy is to always take two frogs. Another student may say that she always takes the same number of frogs as her partner. Do not be concerned. With experience, more effective strategies will emerge.

7. Again, use your signal to get the students' attention. Ask if anyone has come up with any new strategies. Add these to the list. As a group, try out one particular strategy. For example, if someone said that a player must go second to win the game, have each pair of students take turns going second. What were the results? Is there conclusive evidence that going second guarantees that a player will win?

8. Stop at this point. Have students continue to play the game at other appropriate times during the week. Keep the list up so they can test strategies and add new findings to the list. Use the large gameboard with the class to try out strategies.

Going Further

1. After students have mastered playing this first version of Frog Pond, try another version of the game. This time the last frog is the "Poison" Frog. Players should try **not** to catch the last frog. How is the game different? What strategies emerge now?

2. Have students write a letter to a friend, famous person, relative, etc. to explain how to catch the "Magic" Frog or how to avoid the "Poison" Frog. Be sure students understand that the person they are writing to knows the game and its rules. The person just wants to know how to win!

3. Send a copy of the gameboard home and have students play with members of their families. They can use beans or other small common household objects. Have the families write up their strategies.

4. Alter the game as follows:

a. Increase the number of frogs in the pond to 12. Does the strategy change? If so, how?

b. Put two Frog Pond boards together so that there are 20 frogs. Now you can also alter the number of frogs that can be caught at one time to 1, 2, or 3! See how the game changes again!

Modifications for Kindergarten

Have the students play the game as described in this session. After the game has been modeled, let the children play the game in pairs. Do not list strategies or attempt to get the whole group to try out a specific strategy. Use the large gameboard at the end to talk about strategies.

Note: Some kindergarten children may have difficulty understanding that it is not the *number* of frogs that one catches, but taking the **last** frog that is important in this game. For example, it may be confusing that although one player caught six frogs, their partner, who only caught four, won because she took the last one. Be sure to point this out.

"The Pond," a computer game by Sunburst for students in grades 2 and beyond, is a wonderful technology connection to the Frog Pond game. As a frog leaps through a maze of lily pads, students try to find the pattern that will get it back to the magic lily pad. *See page 72 for information on how to purchase "The Pond."*

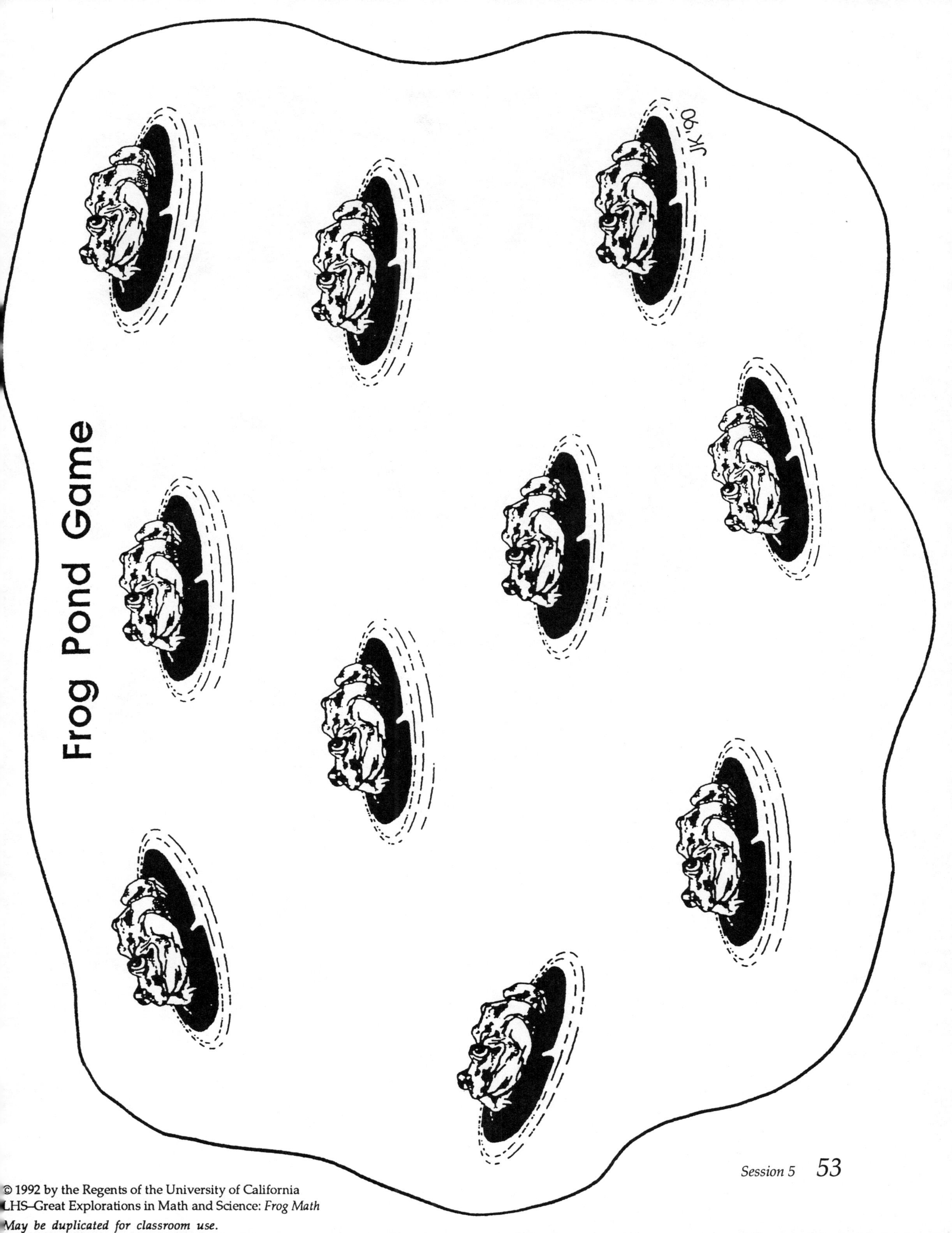
Frog Pond Game

SUPER
MARIO BROS.

Session 6: Hop to the Pond Game

Overview

The Hop to the Pond games delight students as they cheer on frogs that race to a large pond. In the first version of the game, six frogs race to be the first frog to hop into the cool pond. The frogs hop closer and closer to the pond by the roll of a die. Before this race begins, students predict a winner. Next, partners play the game and record the results. Then, these results are analyzed. Did each of the six frogs win the race at least once? Did one frog win more frequently that the other frogs? Is this a fair race?

In a second version of Hop to the Pond, played on a subsequent day, six more frogs are added to the game. Now twelve frogs race to the pond—this time being propelled by the roll of two dice! Again, students predict their personal winners, and then play the game with a partner. Results are recorded and analyzed. Do certain frogs win more frequently than others? Is one frog very lucky, or is there more to it than that? Is this race fair to all the frogs?

The Hop to the Pond games are experiments in ***statistics and probability*** that give young students a context in which they can generate and interpret data. As they play the games and record the results, certain frogs may emerge as winners more frequently than others. Some frogs may never leave the starting line! Children also discover which numbers are more likely to be rolled when one die or two dice are thrown. In addition, the game with twelve frogs provides an enjoyable way to practice the "number facts" from 2 to 12 that can be generated by the dice.

This activity encourages students to: explore statistics and probability with concrete materials; calculate "number facts" to 12; develop strategies to make likely predictions; collect and interpret data; work cooperatively and play fairly.

What You Need

For the class:

- ❒ large gameboard with 6 frogs from pages 96–97 (Part 1)
- ❒ large gameboard with 12 frogs from pages 98–99 (Part 2)
- ❒ 1 large pair of dice, 2"–5" cubes. Several sources for dice are listed on page 72.
- ❒ 12 small plastic frogs or other markers
- ❒ 1 pad of "post-its" 2" x 1 1/2"
- ❒ 1 set of felt markers
- ❒ rubber cement
- ❒ 2 pieces of 12" x 18" tagboard or matté board
- ❒ 18 sheets of letter size (8 1/2" x 11") paper (or card stock) on which to duplicate the student gameboard with 6 frogs
- ❒ 18 sheets of legal size (8 1/2" x 14") paper (or card stock) on which to duplicate the student gameboard with 12 frogs
- ❒ *(optional)* laminator or clear contact paper

For each pair of students:

- ❒ 1 student gameboard with 6 frogs (Part 1)
- ❒ 1 student gameboard with 12 frogs (Part 2)
- ❒ 2 dice
- ❒ 12 small plastic frogs or other markers
- ❒ 1 cup or other container for frogs
- ❒ *(optional)* plastic "strawberry" basket

Getting Ready

1. If you have second or third graders, decide whether you will have them write their descriptions of dice during this session. (See **"For second and third grade students"** on page 58.) If you want them to write during a separate period or for homework, you will need to model the Hop to the Pond game **after** they have had time to write the letter.

2. Color in the large gameboards with marking pens. Use rubber cement to attach each board to a piece of tagboard or matté board. *Optional:* Cover with clear contact paper or laminate.

3. Duplicate the student-size gameboard with 6 frogs from page 65 on letter size (8 1/2" x 11") paper or card stock and

the student-size gameboard with 12 frogs from pages 66–67 on legal size (8 1/2" x 14") paper or card stock. If possible, duplicate on different colors to further differentiate the two games.

4. Arrange tables so that pairs can work together.

a. For the first day, put a student gameboard with 6 frogs, a cup filled with 6 small frogs, and one die at each work space.

b. On the day that you play the version of the game with 12 frogs, put a student gameboard with 12 frogs, a cup filled with 12 small frogs, and two dice at each work space.

5. Prepare a table on the chalkboard.

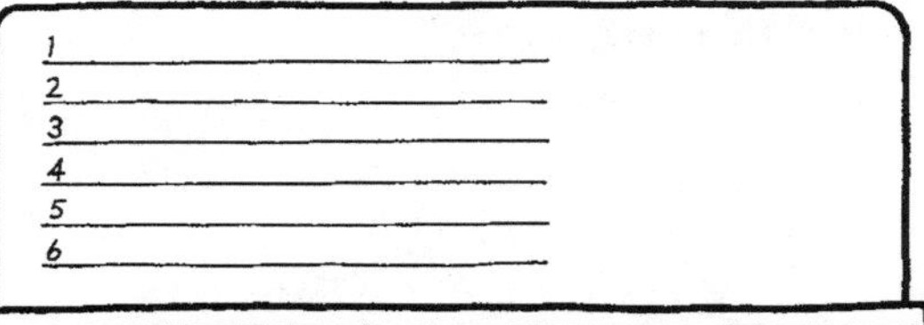

a. Just before you teach the game with 6 frogs, write the numbers 1 through 6 on the chalkboard. Make each numeral about 2" high so that the "post-its" will fit easily next to the numbers. Draw lines between the numbers.

b. On the day that you teach the version of the game with 12 frogs, write the numbers 1 through 12 on the chalkboard and proceed as you did above for the game with 6 frogs.

6. Gather the materials.

a. On the first day that you play the game, gather the large gameboard with 6 frogs, 6 small frogs, 1 large die, and a copy of the student gameboard.

b. On the day that you play the version of the game with 12 frogs, gather the large gameboard with 12 frogs, 12 small frogs, 2 large dice, and a copy of the student gameboard.

7. *Optional:* Have a copy of *Jumanji* by Chris Van Allsberg and *Frog and Toad Are Friends* available.

Part 1: Hop to the Pond—6 Frogs Race! (Grades K–3)

Modeling the Game with the Whole Class

If you're playing the game with kindergarten students, be sure to read "Modifications for Kindergarten" on page 63.

1. Gather students in a circle in an area away from their desks.

a. **For kindergarten and first grade**, begin by asking students what they know about dice. If they have difficulty responding, ask leading questions, such as: *What numbers are on each die?* [1–6] *How are the numbers represented?* [Usually with dots] *What shape are the faces on the die?* [Square] *What shape is the die?* [Cube] *What games have you played that use dice? How are the dice used in these games?* (If it seems that many students have never used dice before, begin by giving each student one. Let them find out all they can about the die before playing the game.)

Be sure to allow ample time to write the letter. You may want to use another period for this part of the activity or have the students write it for a homework assignment. If you do, then begin the lesson by listening to the letters.

b. **For second and third grade students**, begin by asking students to write you a letter. They are to pretend that you are from another planet. You have never seen dice before. Ask them to write you a letter that describes dice. Tell them to write as much as possible because you are very interested in learning about dice. Give students about ten minutes to write. Then listen to a few letters. Record information that you "learn" about dice as they read their letters.

Dear Jaine
dis are Skwar
and we yoos
them for roling
hubers
thv got nubers
on ech side
thv got nubers
1 2 3 4 5 6
from Rebecca

Dear Jame,
The things I know about dice is you play games with them. Thay have dots on them so you know what numbers ~~thay~~ are. And then you roll them from your hands. And it is a square dices. Also they have 6 sides. Used all over the world. Used a lot in Reno. 21 on one die.
From Melissa

2. Let the children know that they are going to use a die to play a frog race game called Hop to the Pond.

3. Show the students the large gameboard. Ask the children to pretend that it is a hot day and the frogs are all racing to get to the cool pond. Each frog wants to get there first. Place 6 frogs on the numbered frogs pictured on the board. Ask, *How many frogs are racing?* [6]

4. Before explaining anything else about the game, ask students to predict which frog will get to the pond first. Ask for a show of hands as you call out each number.

5. Roll the large die. Ask the children what the top number is on the die. Explain that the frog whose number corresponds to the number on the top face of the die can move forward **one** space. (In many games that use dice, the number rolled corresponds to the number of spaces a playing piece can move. That is **not** the case in this game.)

6. Give the die to the child on your left side. Have her roll the die. Let the child on your right side move the frog which corresponds to the number rolled forward one space. Pass the die around the circle to the next person on the left. He rolls. What is the number this time? Continue around the circle on the right side. On this side, the next child moves the appropriate frog forward one space. Continue passing the die around the circle and moving the frog until one frog wins the race.

7. Ask questions during the course of the game, such as: *Which frog is in the lead (winning)? Are any frogs still at the starting point? How many hops has Frog 3 taken so far? How many more hops until Frog 2 gets to the pond? Are any frogs tied in the race? Do you want to change your prediction? Why?*

8. Play until one frog wins the race. Ask more questions: *Why did that frog win the race? Which frog(s) came in second? Were any frogs far behind in the race?*

Playing Hop to the Pond with a Partner

1. Let the children know that they are going to play the game with a partner using a similar board. Show a student gameboard. Compare it with the large gameboard. Model how to play a game with a child partner. Place 6 small frogs on the board with your partner. Take turns rolling the dice and moving the frogs. When only two are playing, it works well to have the person both roll and move the frog. Take turns doing this a few times so that everyone understands how to play with a partner.

One teacher recommended that students roll the dice into plastic strawberry baskets to decrease the sounds of the dice being tossed on table tops as well as to contain the dice.

2. Explain to the students that after they've played the game and they have a winner, they should come to the chalkboard. They will write the number of the frog that won their race on a "post-it," and put the "post-it" on the chalkboard next to the same number. Those students can go back and play the game again.

3. Have students choose partners and go to designated areas to play the game. Circulate to see how the game is progressing. Assist students as they put their "post-its" on the chalkboard.

4. When you are sure that all students have finished at least one game, collect the game materials. Focus attention on the chalkboard. Examine the data. Begin by counting how many "post-its" are next to each number, 1 through 6. Record the number of "post-its" next to each number. If a frog did not win any races, write a zero next to that frog's

number. Ask questions to help the class interpret the data, such as: *Which frog won the most races? Which frog won the fewest races? Did any frog not win a race? Do you think that this is a fair race for all the frogs? Why or why not?*

NOTE: In this version of the game, all the frogs stand an equal chance of winning the game. (See the "For Teachers Only" section for an explanation of the probability involved.) However, the children are learning about dice as well as gathering and analyzing data. It is important to listen to and acknowledge their observations as well as to listen to their reasoning and thinking processes. **Resist the temptation to explain the data any further than your students suggest.**

5. Make the game available to the children at appropriate times. Keep an on-going record of the frogs that win each race.

Part 2: Hop to the Pond—Now 12 Frogs Race! (Grades 1–3)

Modeling the Game with the Whole Class

1. Gather students in a circle in an area away from their desks.

2. Tell students that the Hop to the Pond game is going to have 6 new frogs added to the race. Show the new large gameboard. Place 12 frogs on the numbered frogs pictured on the board.

3. Ask students to predict which frog will get to the pond first in this new version of the game. Ask for a show of hands as you call out each number.

4. Tell students that two dice will be used to move the frogs. Roll the pair of large dice. Ask the children what the top number is on each die. Ask, *What is the sum of the two numbers rolled?* Explain that the frog whose number corresponds to the sum of the dice can move forward **one** space in a similar way that the frogs moved in the first game.

5. Model how to move the frog whose number corresponds to the sum of the two dice. Let the children know that you will be the person to move the frogs in this first race, and that they will roll the dice to determine which frog will hop a space.

6. Pass one die to the student on each side of you. Have these two students roll the dice next. What is the sum of the numbers on the dice? Which frog can move? How many spaces can that frog move? Move the frog whose number corresponds to the sum **one** space.

7. Have each of the two students pass their die to the person next to them. These students then roll the dice.

8. Point out a counting strategy to use with the dice. For example, if a five and a six are rolled, point to the six and have children say that number. Then point to the die with five dots and count on to eleven.

9. After about eight rolls, ask questions, such as: *Which frog is ahead? Are any frogs tied in the race? Are any frogs still waiting to go? Would you like to change your prediction? WHY?*

10. Continue rolling until each student has rolled one die. *It is not important to finish the race!* The purpose of playing this version of the game as a group is to model how to use two dice and move the frog. Ask for more observations about the race at this point. If the interest is high and/or an outcome to the race is imminent, finish the game. If not, move on to the partner activity.

Playing Hop to the Pond with a Partner

1. As in the previous game, students play with a partner using the student gameboard. Choose a student partner. Model how to set up and play part of a game with a partner. Place 12 small frogs on the board. Take turns rolling both dice. Find the sum together. The person who rolled moves the frog one space. Take turns with your partner. To be sure students understand, ask for a volunteer to review how to play the game.

2. Students follow the same procedure with this version of the game as in Part 1. After a frog wins the race, they record the number of the winner on a "post-it," and put the "post-it" on the chalkboard next to the corresponding number. Those students can go back and play the game again.

3. Circulate to see how the game is progressing. Assist students as necessary.

4. When you are sure that all students have finished at least one game, collect the game materials. Focus attention on the chalkboard. Examine the data. Begin by counting how many "post-its" are next to each number, 1 through 12. Record the number of "post-its" next to each number. If a frog did not win any races, write a zero next to that frog's number. Ask questions to help the class interpret the data, such as: *Did any frog(s) stay at the starting line? Why didn't they move? Is it possible for them to move? Which frog(s) won the race the most times? How many times? Which frog(s) came in second place? Why do you think that one frog won more races? Do you think that this is a fair frog race? Why or why not?*

5. After only one round of playing this game, students may not have answers to many of these questions. They may not yet understand the reasons why the frogs moved in the ways that they did. For example, they may think that one frog is lucky and that is why it won. Some students may say that the reason a frog won more frequently was because that number was rolled more times. That is an accurate observation and it is the first step in

explaining the results of the game. **Resist the temptation to explain the data any further than your students suggest.** Let them play the game more times to discover that certain frogs are more likely to win more than other frogs.

6. If a student does come up with an important, accurate observation, be sure to allow her to explain her thinking to the group. For example, she might say that Frog One can never leave the starting line. Ask her why. She may tell the class that it is impossible to roll a "one" using two dice! By listening to your students' thinking, you will gain insight into their levels of understanding. Proceed at their pace.

Going Further

This activity is appropriate for students from kindergarten through third grade. It provides another opportunity for students to gain information about dice through experimentation and data gathering.

1. Try another experiment with the die called "Roll All Six." Have students predict how many times they will need to roll a die to get each of the six numbers to come up one time. Students then take a die and a recording sheet (see page 64) to conduct the experiment. Make a data chart of the results. Ask questions about their results, such as: *What is the fewest number of rolls it took? What is the largest number of rolls it took? What number of rolls did most people take to get all six numbers? What is the fewest number of rolls it could take a person to roll all six? What is the largest number of rolls it could take a person to roll all six?*

2. Have students continue to play the Hop to the Pond game with 12 frogs at other times. Keep an on-going data chart to record the race results. With more experience using the dice, it is likely that your students will begin to draw accurate conclusions about the dice. Some may understand the reason that Frogs Six, Seven, and Eight win more frequently than the other frogs in the race with 12 frogs.

3. Fair and Unfair: Ask your students if they think that the Hop to the Pond games are fair or unfair. Have them explain their thinking. If the game is unfair, challenge them to change the game so that it is fair.

4. The book *Jumanji* by Chris Van Allsburg connects well with this session. The book is the name of a board game that two children find when they are bored. The game uses dice to move players and the toss of the dice is crucial as the game progresses. You may want to have students predict the likelihood of rolling the numbers that the children roll—especially at the end of the game.

5. Ask second and third grade students to pretend that they are going to a frog race in which 12 frogs are racing. Tell them that they have $100 to bet on a frog. Which frog would they bet on to win? Have them explain why. In addition, is there any frog that they would bet on to *lose* the race? Why? If you would prefer not to introduce any issues related to gambling, you could have students pretend they are buying one frog to enter the race. Which one would they buy if they wanted to be likely to win? to lose?

6. You may want to read the Frog and Toad story, "The Swim" (also from *Frog and Toad Are Friends*) in conjunction with this final session. In the story, Frog and Toad go to the river for a swim. Although Toad is the first to admit that he looks very silly in his bathing suit, he still likes to wear it. But Toad does not want anyone to see him in his suit! Students delight in this story, especially as they join a large audience from the story and see Toad emerge from the water in his bathing suit. And he does look quite funny!

my choice is frog bet number 7 because it's the one that is winning the most

I would not pick 1 because number 1 will not win

Modifications for Kindergarten

At the kindergarten level, play only the game in Part 1 Hop to the Pond—6 Frogs Race! Follow the activity as described until it is time to record the numbers of the winning frog. Then, post the large gameboard in the room. Children play until one frog wins. Then have the children raise their hands so a teacher or classroom assistant can come to their gameboard. That person has "post-its" so she can write the number of the winning frog and have children place it on the large gameboard. Students continue to play until all their classmates have had a frog win the race. Proceed with the debriefing questions that are appropriate to your students' abilities and understanding. Resist the urge to explain the game to them. You will be amazed at how long their interest lasts in this game!

vote for number 7,

100 dollars if you pick 7. 1,000,000,000 people vote for 7, everyday! number 7, is gonna win because it exersised and it pumpad weight and it ran everyday and it went to the jym!

In this version of the game, the children practice counting skills, connect a written number with the number of dots or numeral on the die and move the frog that corresponds to the number on the die only one space. They also gain experience following directions, cooperating with a partner, and are introduced to statistics and probability.

ROLL ALL SIX

1. Guess how many times you need to throw the die before you see every number come up.

Write down your guess: ☐

2. Now, throw the die and make a check mark for the number that comes up. Keep doing this until every number has come up.

⚀ ______

⚁ ______

⚂ ______

⚃ ______

⚄ ______

⚅ ______

3. Add up all the check marks. How close was your guess to this number?

Hop To The Pond!

1							1
2							2
3							3
4							4
5							5
6							6

Hop To
1
2
3
4
5
6
1
2
3
4
5
6
1
2
3
4
5
6

The Pond!
7
8
9
10
11
12
7
8
9
10
11
12
7
8
9
10
11
12

FOR TEACHERS ONLY

Background Information on Probability, Statistics, and Dice

One Die: When only one die is used, all six numbers on the die have an equal chance of being rolled. Played many times, the Hop to the Pond game with six frogs and one die usually can illustrate that no one number occurs more frequently than any other number. With a small amount of data, one number may occur more frequently than other numbers. However, as the die experiment is done a large number of times, the distribution of the numbers one through six is likely to be quite even.

One second grade student told us that each number on one die has a "partner" on the other die to make seven. She said this is not the case with the other sums.

Two Dice: The chart below shows the possible combinations that can be rolled when throwing two dice—this relates to the Hop to the Pond game with twelve frogs and two dice. Use dice of two different colors to help illustrate that the same sum of two numbers can be rolled different ways. For example, a six can be rolled with a red two and a blue four as well as with a red four and a blue two.

	⚀	⚁	⚂	⚃	⚄	⚅
⚀	2	3	4	5	6	7
⚁	3	4	5	6	7	8
⚂	4	5	6	7	8	9
⚃	5	6	7	8	9	10
⚄	6	7	8	9	10	11
⚅	7	8	9	10	11	12

By looking at this chart, one can note that the number 7 occurs most frequently and that the 7s form a diagonal on the chart. The number 7 can be made with many different combinations of numbers on the dice, so that frog has the most chances to win. After 7, the numbers 6 and 8 occur equally frequently and only one less time than 7. Therefore, it is also quite probable that one of these two frogs will win the race. The numbers 2 and 12 can only be rolled one way! It is very unlikely that frog 2 or 12 would win the race.

Despite the varying probabilities that each frog will win, any of the frogs *could* win the race, except frog number 1. (Using two dice, it is impossible for the number 1 to be rolled.) The ***probability*** is that number 7 will be rolled most frequently; therefore frog number 7 will win most games, but the other frogs do have a *possibility* of winning!

Sample Letter Requesting Buttons

Dear Families,

We will soon begin a new mathematics unit, *Frog Math: Predict, Ponder, Play*. Your child will be working with a variety of hands-on materials including buttons, beans, and plastic frogs, to develop skills such as: observation, prediction, description, classification, estimation, recording data, and logical thinking. The engaging activities and games in this unit also integrate literature, art, and writing.

There are several household items that that we will need for this unit. For the first two sessions, we will be investigating buttons. The buttons will be used by the children to do a variety of math activities that include sorting and classifying, playing logic games and graphing. **Any buttons** that you could donate would be greatly appreciated. Buttons with unusual attributes (three holes, square, ceramic, etc.) would enrich the collection.

I am looking forward to starting this exciting and fun unit on _____(day and date)__________. It would be most helpful for your child to begin to bring in the buttons *before* that date. Even after the unit has started, additional buttons will still be appreciated!

Thanks for your help and support with this project.

Sample Letter for Going Further Collecting and Sorting Activities

Dear Families,

We are well underway with our mathematics unit, *Frog Math: Predict, Ponder, Play.* The children had great fun working with the buttons and learning about attributes. To continue our exploration, we are collecting additional household items for a set of "class junk" or "treasure boxes." Each box will contain an assortment of one item such as: *old keys, bottle caps, rocks, shells, nuts and bolts, screws, seeds, plastic bread tags, etc.* **Please note that none of the items needs to be purchased**. These collections help children see how to recycle and use materials in new and different ways.

I have asked the children to look at home and outdoors for a few of the items mentioned above to donate to the class collections. Attached is a small square of paper to be used as a measuring tool. Any item that your child brings in must be able to fit inside the square. Lastly, keep in mind that these items will remain at school in the boxes, so *please be sure that anything your child brings in will not be missed!*

Your child can begin bringing in the items s/he wants to contribute on ______(day and date)______.

Thanks for your continued help and support with this project!

Sources for Materials

Buttons

Buttons are used in Session 1 (free exploration of buttons and the "Button Up" and "Button Factory" games) and Session 2 (button sorting).

Creative Publications
50400 West 11th Street
Oak Lawn, IL 60453
(800) 624-0822

An assortment of buttons in varying sizes, colors, and numbers of holes. Sold by weight: 3/4 pound. Comes in a 6" x 6" plastic box for storage. **Cost:** $11.50 (#31062 Buttons Collection)

Cuisenaire Company of America, Inc.
10 Bank Street
White Plains, NY 10602
(800) 237-3142

Buttons by the Pound come in assorted sizes and colors with the number of button holes varying from 2–4 holes. Approximately 1000 pieces. **Cost:** $9.95 (#029114)

Lakeshore Learning Materials
2695 E. Dominguez Street
P.O. Box 6261
Carson, CA 90749
(800) 421-5354

Over 500 assorted buttons in all kinds of textures, shapes, and sizes. Diameters vary from 1/4" to 1 1/4". Sold by weight: 1 pound bag. **Cost:** $6.95 (#AB920)

Note: **Prices listed are subject to change. Please confirm current prices and other information with all suppliers before ordering.**

Small Plastic Frogs

Small plastic frogs are used for estimation activities in Session 4, in the Frog Pond game (Session 5), and the Hop to the Pond game (Session 6).

CONCEPTS TO GO (Mail Order Only)
Box 10043
Berkeley, CA 94709
(510) 848-3233
FAX: (510) 486-1248

Small, dark green frogs, in a seated position, measuring 1/2" long by 3/4" high. There are 60 frogs in a bag at $9.95 per bag. If you want a LOT of frogs, you can purchase them by the gross (144), minimum of 6 gross, at $13.95 per gross. Concepts to Go does not accept orders for under $15.00.

Ideal School Supply
110 S. Lavergne Avenue
Oak Lawn, IL 60453
(800) 845-8149

Small 1" frogs in red, blue, green, and yellow are available in sets that are listed under "Animal Counters." Set of 100 frogs is $11.95 (#30836B) and set of 300 frogs is $35.00 (#30837B).

U.S. Toy Company, Inc.
1227 East 119th Street
Grandview, MO 64030
(800) 255-6124
FAX: (816) 761-9295

These frogs are 2" long and come in an assortment of colors including yellow, green, blue, and red. The frogs have an added feature of being able to "jump" when pushed down on their "tails." You could have fun doing measurement activities with these jumpers, in addition to the other games and activities in this guide. **Cost:** 144 for $2.50 (#125C).

Large Frogs (and Toads)

Discovery Corner LHS*
Lawrence Hall of Science
U.C. Berkeley, CA 94720
(510) 642-1016

The Discovery Corner carries a toad that works as a good substitute for a large frog. It is made out of rubber and measures 3 1/2" in length and 2 1/2" in width. The toad is a dark, olive green, has protruding eyes and a bumpy body. It looks quite realistic! **Cost**: $1.75 for each "Wildlife Artist Toad" (ask for it by this name).

Archie McPhee
P.O. Box 30852
Seattle, WA 98103
(206) 782-2344

Big Squeak Frog is a smooth green tree frog that measures over 5" long and can squeak. Works very well for modeling the frog games with large boards. **Cost**: $2.25 each (#9840)

Bright Green Tree Frogs are a miniature version of the large Big Squeak Frog without the squeak. Measures about 2" long. Can also be used for modeling games. **Cost**: 10 for $6.25 (#9833)

Dice

Dice are used in Session 6, the Hop to the Pond game.

Lakeshore Learning Materials
2695 E. Dominguez Street
P.O. Box 6261
Carson, CA 90749
(800) 421-5354

Giant Sponge Number Dice LC711. These are good for modeling the large Hop to the Pond game. Each die is 5" cube with 1–6 dots on each face. **Cost:** $6.95/pair

Standard Dice LC11. Each die is 5/8" cube with 1–6 dots on each face. **Cost:** $2.75/for a set of 10.

Creative Publications
50400 West 11th Street
Oak Lawn, IL 60453
(800) 624-0822

These dice are made of highly polished, true cut, drilled and spotted catalin. Designed for probability experiments and games.

Each 1/2" die is a cube with 1–6 dots on the faces.
Cost: $4.25 for 12 dice (#38239)
$21.00 for 72 dice—24 red, 24 green, 12 white (#38241)

Each 5/8" die is a cube with 1–6 dots on the faces.
Cost: $4.50 for 12 dice (#38242)
$23.75 for 72 dice—24 red, 24 green, 12 white (#38243)

Math Learning Center
P.O. Box 3226
Salem, OR 97302
(503) 370-8130

This company sells **foam** cubes that can be made into *silent* dice. They are available in four sizes. **Cost**: $ 1.25 for a bag of any one of the following: twenty 1 1/2" cubes (CF 150); sixteen 2" cubes (CF 200); four 3" cubes (CF 300); or two 4" cubes (CF 400).

Computer Game

This makes a great connection to the Frog Pond game in Session 5.

Sunburst Communications
101 Castleton Street
P.O. Box 100
Pleasantville, NY 10570-0100
(800) 321-7511
FAX: (914) 747-4109

See sidebar on page 51 for a description of the game "The Pond." Versions are available for Apple II and Macintosh computers as well as Windows 3.1 (or higher) and IBM computers. The cost varies with system used.

Literature Connections

Alligator Shoes
by Arthur Dorros
E.P. Dutton, New York. 1982
Grades: Preschool–2

Being locked in a shoe store by mistake is Alvin Alligator's dream come true. He tries on an endless variety of footwear, but his decision about what footgear he prefers will surprise and delight your students. Great to read before having students use their own shoes to sort (as in Session 2) and use as the data for a real-life graph.

Buster Loves Buttons
by Fran Manushkin, illustrations by Dirk Zimmer
Harper & Row, New York. 1985
Grades: K–3

In this "I Can Read" book, Buster— the button glutton—gets his come-uppance and, in the end, Buster and the rest of the world are happy sorting billions of buttons. Nice introduction to the idea that sorting can be interesting and fun!

The Button Blanket: An Activity Book
A Northwest Coast Indian Art Series
by Nan McNutt, Design and illustration by Yasu Osawa
Northwest Coast Art by Nancy Dawson
Nan McNutt/P.O. Box 295/Petersburg, Alaska 99833

Activity book for Grades K–4 that combines buttons and blankets with Native American art and design. Even the cover is part of an activity.

The Button Box
by Margarette S. Reid; illustrated by Sarah Chamberlain
Dutton's Children's Books, New York. 1992
Grades: Preschool–2

As a young child explores and examines buttons in Grandma's special button box, he sorts and classifies them. Many attributes are illustrated, including color and size, materials buttons are made from, and buttons for different articles of clothing. This is a wonderful springboard to directed sorting in Session 2: Sort, Classify, and "Guess the Sort." Buttons are also used to make a toy and create eyes on a puppet. A brief history of buttons for adults is in the back of the book. This book is also available in Spanish.

A Chair For My Mother/Something Special For Me/
Music, Music for Everyone
by Vera B. Williams
Greenwillow Books, New York. 1982; 1983; 1984
(Also available in paperback from Mulberry Books, New York.)
Grades: K–3

In the first story in this trilogy, a child, her waitress mother, and her grandmother save coins in a large jar to buy a comfortable armchair after all their furniture is lost in a fire. In subsequent stories, Rosa uses coins from the jar to buy an accordion and in the third book uses the accordion to make money for her grandma's medical expenses. As a follow-up, students can estimate how many coins are in a jar and then sort and count small coins. Connects well to Session 4, Frog Guesstimation.

Corduroy
by Don Freeman
The Viking Press, New York. 1968
Grades: Preschool–2

Corduroy, an adventurous teddy bear, wanders around his department store home in search of his lost button. After he is returned to the toy display, a little girl buys him with the pennies she has saved. She sews a new button on his overalls as soon as she gets him home.

The Frog
by Angela Royston; illustrated by Bernard Robinson
Ideals Children's Books, Nashville, Tennessee. 1989
Grades: K–3

Explains the life cycle of a frog through the seasons, beginning with mating in spring. Illustrates predator and prey relationships among animals in a pond habitat. Provides a sampling of the diversity of frogs around the world. Scientific information on frogs and a short glossary are included.

The Frog Alphabet Book…and other awesome amphibians
by Jerry Pallotta; illustrated by Ralph Masiello
Charlesbridge Publishing, Watertown, Massachusetts. 1990
Grades: K–3

A beautifully illustrated book that shows the diversity of amphibians all around the world.

Frog and Toad Are Friends
by Arnold Lobel
Harper & Row, New York. 1970
Grades: K–2

This well-known collection of stories provides the "jumping off place" for *Frog Math* activities. The story "A Lost Button" begins the button sorting and classification session and "The Swim" is often read with the Hop to the Pond game. The entire book is a strong example of how mathematics and literature can be "leapfrogged" together in fun and stimulating ways. This book is now also available in Spanish.

Hippity Hop, Frog on Top
by Natasha Wing; illustrated by DeLoss McGraw
Simon & Schuster, New York. 1994
Grades: K–2

Ten curious frogs trying to see what is on the side of a wall illustrate the numbers from one to ten. Bright, bold illustrations match the frog-counting text and surprise ending. Good connection to Session 4, Frog Guesstimation.

How Much Is A Million?
by David M. Schwartz; illustrated by Steven Kellogg
Lothrop, Lee & Shepard Books, New York. 1985
Grades: K–5

With detailed, whimsical illustrations that include children, goldfish, and stars, this book leads the reader to conceptualize what at first seems inconceivable—a million, a billion, and a trillion. Gives young children as concrete a representation of large numbers as possible. An adult-level explanation to calculate the numbers is included at the end of the book. Ties in well with Session 4, Frog Guesstimation.

Jumanji
by Chris Van Allsburg
Houghton Mifflin, Boston. 1981
Scholastic, New York. 1988
Grades: K–5

A bored brother and sister left on their own find a discarded board game (called Jumanji) which turns their home into an exotic jungle. A final roll of the dice for two sixes helps them escape from an erupting volcano. Goes along well with Session 6: Hop to the Pond game with 12 frogs racing to the pond.

The Magic Bubble Trip
by Ingrid and Dieter Schubert
Kane/Miller Book Publishers, Brooklyn, New York and La Jolla, California. 1985
Grades: K–3

James blows a giant bubble that carries him away to a land of large, hairy frogs where he has a fun, fanciful adventure.

More Than One
by Miriam Schlein, pictures by Donald Crews
Greenwillow Books, New York. 1996
Grades: K–3

Can one be more than one? Absolutely! Using examples, such as two shoes in a pair and seven days in a week, students can see that one "thing" can be a set of more than one. This ties in with the place value activities in which students make groups of tens while working in our base ten number system.

One Hundred Frogs & Ten Flies; Count & Find Series
illustrated by Polly Jordan
McClanahan Book Company, New York. 1992
Grades: Preschool–2

Count by tens all the way to 100 with this delightful, whimsical frog counting book. Added attraction is a hidden fly to find on each page. Connects well with Session 4, Frog Guesstimation.

Only One
by Marc Harshman, illustrated by Barbara Garrison
Dutton Children's Books, New York. 1993
Grades: K–3

At a county fair, the many ways that the number one can be represented are illustrated, from 100 squares on one quilt to twelve eggs in one dozen. Connects with the place value activities in which one ten always has ten ones—just as one dime always has 10 pennies. This book can be used as a springboard to investigate bases other than 10.

The Secret Birthday Message
by Eric Carle
Harper & Row, New York. 1972
Grades: Preschool–2

Instead of a birthday package, Tim gets a mysterious letter written in code. Full-color pages, designed with cut-out shapes, allow children to fully participate in this enticing adventure and follow the trail of shapes in search of the birthday gift. An exciting way to open a shape unit that can include a project to make shape books.

Shoes
by Elizabeth Winthrop, illustrated by William Joyce
Harper & Row, New York. 1986
Grades: Preschool–2

A survey of the many kinds of shoes in the world concludes that the best of all are the perfect natural shoes that are your feet. Great to read before doing a survey of shoes or sorting and classifying a group of real shoes.

Snap, Button, Zip: Inventions to Keep Your Clothes On
by Vicki Cobb, pictures by Marilyn Hafner
HarperCollins, New York. 1989
Grades: K–3

This humorous and informative book has a very nice section on buttons.

A String of Beads
by Margarette S. Reid, pictures by Ashley Wolff
Dutton Children's Books, New York. 1997
Grades: K–4

This gorgeously illustrated book surveys beads, bead collecting, and bead creations from Native American times to the present as a girl and her grandmother do bead work together. As in the author's earlier book on buttons (see *The Button Box* above) this book make a great real-world connection to sorting and classification activities. A background section contains even more interesting information about beads through the ages.

The Stupids Step Out/The Stupids Have a Ball/The Stupids Die
by Harry Allard; illustrated by James Marshall
Houghton Mifflin, Boston. 1974; 1978; 1981
Grades: K–3

These three books about the Stupid family have children laughing with delight as they see the Stupid children do such silly things as slide up a banister or take a bath fully clothed in an empty bath tub. These books promote logical-thinking skills as kids find all the outrageous things and suggest ways to correct them. Ties in with Session 5 as logical thinking helps catch the magic frog!

Tuesday
by David Wiesner
Clarion Books, New York. 1991
Grades: K–Adult

Frogs rise on their lily pads, float through the air, and explore the nearby houses while the inhabitants sleep. Beautifully illustrated almost wordless book.

Whose Hat Is That?
by Ron Roy; photographs by Rosemarie Hausherr
Clarion Books/Ticknor and Fields, New York. 1987
Grades: Preschool–3

Text and photographs portray the appearance and function of 18 types of hats including a top hat, a jockey's cap, and a football helmet. The children and adults modeling the hats represent a rainbow of peoples. Makes a nice connection to the classification activities in Session 2. Children can bring in hats and sort them!

Whose Shoes Are These?
by Ron Roy; photographs by Rosemarie Hausherr
Clarion Books/Ticknor and Fields, New York. 1988
Grades: Preschool–3

Text and photographs portray the appearance and function of 19 types of shoes and footwear. As in the book above, the children and adults modeling the hats represent a rainbow of peoples. Can lead to a sorting and classifying activity with children's shoes as in Session 2.

Assessment Suggestions

Selected Student Outcomes

1. Students demonstrate their understanding that objects have a variety of attributes and may be sorted in many ways. They are able to make observations, sort and classify objects, and record and interpret their observations.

2. Students apply number sense to make reasonable estimates.

3. Students learn what a strategy is and are able to describe strategies that they use. They use logical reasoning to define, verbalize, test, generalize, and refine their strategies.

4. Students are able to recognize that probability is directly related to mathematical patterns that occur when one die and two dice are rolled.

Built-In Assessment Activities

Button Factory: In Session 1, students describe a button for their partner to draw. The teacher can observe how students use vocabulary to articulate attributes, how they listen to their partners' descriptions, and their ability to transfer the description to create a picture. (Outcome 1)

Guess the Sort: In Session 2, groups of students sort buttons and record their methods of classification. Then, they observe other groups and guess how their classmates sorted the buttons. The teacher observes how well students sort the buttons, how accurately they articulate their own methods of sorting, and how they use language and logical reasoning. (Outcome 1)

Dice Pre-Assessment: In Session 6, students tell or write what they know about dice before they play the Hop To The Pond game. From this activity, the teacher can gain a sense of students' knowledge and misconceptions about dice. The teacher can use this information to adjust the lesson so that it is appropriate to the students' experience level. (Outcome 4)

Additional Assessment Ideas

Estimation Station: In a Going Further activity following Session 4, students focus on a weekly estimation station, at which estimates are collected throughout the week. At the end of the week, before the actual unveiling and counting, the teacher may have the students write about which estimate they think is the closest, and why. The teacher can observe students' ability to make and articulate their estimates. (Outcome 2)

Write a Letter: In the Going Further activity that follows Session 5, students write (or dictate) a letter to tell a friend or famous person about how to win the Frog Pond game. The teacher can assess how clearly the students understand the workings of the game, as well as how thoroughly they can articulate their strategies for winning. (Outcome 3)

Betting on the Winning Frog: In the Going Further activity after the Hop to the Pond game, students write their thoughts about which frog is most likely to win the race. This activity can be used to assess students' understanding of probability and how they apply their knowledge of probability to formulate a winning strategy. (Outcomes 3, 4)

Button Treasure Hunt: Have each student draw a button and put their own name on the back of the button. They then write words or sentences to describe the button on an index card. At the end of a school day, gather all the designed buttons and cards. Hide each button somewhere in your classroom. The next day, give students a card, and challenge them to find the button described on the card. Students can check their accuracy by asking the student whose name appears on the found button. After students have completed the task, have them list the steps they took to find the button, state how they knew it was the correct button, and think of words they could add to the description of the button. (Outcome 1)

> *Please note:* **The Button Treasure Hunt assessment appears as a Case Study with actual student work on page 84 of *Insights and*** *Outcomes: Assessments for Great Explorations in Math and Science,* **also known as the GEMS assessment handbook.**

Estimation Jar: Create an estimation jar with a number of items appropriate to the developmental level of the students. Have the students record their estimate of items on a strip of paper; then pour out the contents of the jar. Have students write a new estimate under their original guess. Next, count out some of the items and have students record a new estimate. Finally, count the remainder of the items and have students write the actual answer. The paper strips will reveal each student's original guess, and how they refined their estimates as more information was provided. (Outcome 2)

Who Goes First?: Present students with the rules to a simple game, such as Tic-Tac-Toe. Ask them to write about whether they would want to go first, or second, and why. (Outcome 3)

Three Dice Hop: Discuss with students what might happen if the Hop To The Pond game were played with three dice. How would the frogs be numbered? Which frogs do they think would win the most often? Why? Have students write about their ideas. They then can play this version of the game, and share their results and insights. (Outcome 4)

Summary Outlines

Session 1: The Lost Button Story

Getting Ready

At least a month before activity, begin a button collection. Obtain *Frog and Toad Are Friends*. Familiarize yourself with "The Lost Button" story. Purchase/make felt board. Cut out felt buttons. Gather: the book, felt board, felt buttons (stacked in order of display). For each pair of students, fill 1 cup with 40–50 buttons of wide variety. If closing with the "Button Factory" game, have sheets of paper and crayons/markers ready.

Reading and Exploring

1. Gather students in group area and read "The Lost Button." Stop at points noted in text and place buttons on felt board. After the story, focus on felt buttons and ask for observations.

2. In pairs, students investigate real buttons. Allow for 10–15 minutes of **free** exploration and circulate. Generate a word list of button attributes. Close with either the "**Button Up**" game (grades 1 and 2) or the "**Button Factory**" game (grades 2 and 3) as detailed in text.

Session 2: Sort, Classify, and "Guess the Sort"

Getting Ready

Decide if you will use the book *The Button Box* to introduce this session. Make a collection of felt buttons as detailed in text. **Be sure there is color contrast so buttons stand out on felt board!** Make large and small yarn loops. Cut three 9" lengths of "sentence strips." Have on hand: felt board, felt buttons from Session 1 and those made for this session, yarn loops, three cards, felt pen, and 3 real buttons (1 small, 1 medium, 1 large). For each pair of students, fill 1 cup with 40–50 buttons.

Sorting, Classifying, and Guessing

1. Gather students in group area. Ask questions to review "The Lost Button." Put large felt buttons from Session 1 on the felt board as children describe them. Give new cups of buttons to new pairs of students. While they explore, replace the felt buttons on board with colored felt buttons.

2. After 5 to 10 minutes, gather in group area and ask what they have discovered about the new buttons.

3. Optional: Read *The Button Box* story to springboard into the sorting activity you choose to do.

Sorting by Color

1. Show felt board with colored felt buttons. Ask for ways to put them in groups. Accept all ideas. Use color as first attribute to sort. Place one small loop around each button group and ask comparison questions about the buttons.

2. Students work with their same partners to sort buttons by color. When they finish, ask each student to choose a favorite button and bring it to group area.

Sorting by Size

1. Tell students you'll put their favorite buttons in groups by size. Hold up large button. Ask children to describe its size. Agree on a word and write that word on a sentence strip. Do the same with medium/small buttons. Label the 3 large yarn loops on floor with word cards and corresponding sample buttons. Ask students to predict which loop will have most buttons after everyone has placed their favorite button in a loop.

2. Fill loops with buttons by asking for buttons of different sizes. Check for agreement of size as buttons are placed. After about half are placed, ask students to predict which loop will have the most when sort is done. Rest of class, one by one, places buttons. Ask for observations. Count buttons in each loop and pose questions to focus on comparisons.

3. Children return to seats to sort buttons by size. When most have completed task, have them "freeze." Ask them to report about the size groups they created.

Inventing New Ways to Sort

1. Return to group area and review how felt buttons were sorted. [Color] Remove loops. Ask students for other ways to sort. Take all suggestions. Choose an attribute and sort buttons.

2. Sort by another attribute. Then partners return to their buttons and sort any way(s) they choose. After 5 minutes, stop work and leave buttons sorted. Partners walk around to see sorts done by classmates and play "Guess the Sort."

Session 3: Designer Buttons

Getting Ready

Make (purchase) a graphing grid and labels for graph as described in text. Duplicate one Button Template master sheet for each student. In work areas, place decoration materials—crayons, markers, colored pencils, pens, scissors, hole punchers. Use masking tape to hang graph on chalkboard. Make masking tape loops, one per student and one per label, and place next to graph.

Designing Buttons

1. Gather students in group area and tell them they'll be button designers. Show them copy of Button Template sheet. Have students name the shapes of the buttons on template sheet. [Triangle, oval, square, circle] Give each student a template. They decorate, cut out and punch up to 4 holes in as many buttons as they can in 15–20 minutes. Choose **one** favorite button and write names/initials on back.

2. Graph their designer buttons according to number of holes. Hold up card labeled "one hole," and ask volunteer to read it. Attach to graph with masking tape loop. Label the other three long rows in the same way. Ask a volunteer to place her button on graphing grid. Does class agree or disagree? Another places button. Does anyone have a button in a different row? Continue until half of students have placed buttons. Predict which row will have the most, fewest.

3. After everyone's button is on graph, listen to observations and ask questions. Take "number of holes" label cards off graph and have students remove their buttons from grid.

4. Label rows with shape cards. Ask students to predict how graph will look. Have them place buttons on graph as above. Ask for observations. Brainstorm other ways to graph buttons. Decide upon a way, make labels for it, and graph. Ask for observations. Continue as interest allows.

Session 4: Frog Guesstimation

Getting Ready

Fill plastic jar with a number of small plastic frogs, as specified in text (by grade level). Duplicate/prepare large place value board and a student place value board for each student. Divide lima beans equally into ziplock bags. **Before day of activity**, show jar of frogs to students. Do not let them open it. **On day of presentation**, gather large place value board and small cups as described in text. Have copy of student place value board, 10 cups, ziplock bags with lima beans, and "post-its" in group area. Put student place value board, 8 cups, dark marker, and "post-it" at student work space.

Part 1: Guesstimating Frogs

1. Volunteers "guesstimate" the number of frogs in jar. As students estimate, they tell how to write the number. **Keep estimates anonymous.** After estimates recorded, ask students for highest/lowest (the ***range***) and circle these. Will actual number of frogs be between these two numbers?

2. How will we find out actual number? [Count frogs!] Show the place value counting board. Point out the tens' side and ones' side on board. Count number of circles on each side. Explain that board will help count the frogs.

3. Open jar and pour out frogs. Reevaluate original estimate from this new perspective. Students make higher/lower/same estimates mentally. Using the place value board, students count with you until the ones' side is filled with frogs. Model how board works: put the 10 frogs in cup and place it on tens' side. How many frogs are on the board? [Ten] Count until ones' side has ten more frogs. Ask what to do next. [Make group of ten, put in cup, and place on tens' side.] How many frogs now on board? [Twenty]

4. Point out frogs on board and those not yet counted. Have students rethink their estimates. Continue counting. Have students make one more mental estimate when pile of uncounted frogs is a dozen or so. Finish counting. Record actual number on board.

5. Compare actual number to estimates. With student input, draw line through estimates that are too large/small. Find estimate(s) that is(are) closest to actual. How far from actual number was estimate? **NOTE: Emphasize this is not a contest—no winners or losers! There are some "closer" answers, but no "wrong" answers.**

Part 2: Guesstimating Handfuls of Lima Beans (Grades 1–3)

1. Draw line down center of chalkboard and label sides "Estimates" and "Actual Number of Beans." Model activity for children with student place value board, lima beans, and paper cups, as in main text, defining a "handful" and writing estimate on chalkboard and actual number on "post-it."

2. Students take handfuls of beans, put beans in a container, and record estimate on chalkboard. As they count beans on place value boards, give students "post-it" to record actual number. After all students have posted their actual number, determine and circle the highest/lowest number (the range) under "Estimates" and "Actual Number of Beans." Make comparisons about these ranges.

3. Focus on data for actual number of beans in a handful. How could the data be organized so it is easy to read and interpret? Try arranging the "post-its" **more than one way**—according to student suggestions. Discuss for as long as time and interest allow.

Session 5: The Frog Pond Game

Getting Ready

Color and prepare Frog Pond gameboard as detailed in text. Obtain 10 large plastic frogs. For each pair of students, duplicate a student-size gameboard and fill a small paper cup with ten small plastic frogs. Gather all material in group area.

Playing Frog Pond

1. Gather students in group area. Introduce Frog Pond game and gameboard. Explain game and ask for volunteer to play game with you. Play until one player takes last frog. Play another full game with *same* student.

2. Show student-sized Frog Pond gameboard/frogs and have students play game with partner. After 10–15 minutes, stop play. Ask how many students have won a game. Does anyone have a strategy (plan) to catch the magic frog? List strategies on butcher paper.

3. Students go back to their games. Has anyone come up with new strategies? Add to list. As a group, try out one strategy. Have students play game during week; keep listing strategies. Cross out ones that are proven inaccurate.

Session 6: Hop to the Pond Games

Getting Ready

As homework or during separate period, have second or third grade students write letter describing dice. Prepare large gameboards as in text. As described in text, for each pair of students, duplicate one copy of student gameboard with 6 frogs and one copy of student gameboard with 12 frogs.

When teaching game with 6 frogs, put student gameboard with 6 frogs, cup filled with 6 frogs, and one die at each work space for each pair of students. Write numbers 1 through 6 on chalkboard and draw lines between numbers. Gather large gameboard with 6 frogs, 6 frogs, one die, and copy of student gameboard. Optional: *Jumanji* and *Frog and Toad Are Friends*.

When teaching game with 12 frogs, put student gameboard with 12 frogs, cup filled with 12 frogs, and two dice at each work space for each pair of students. Write numbers 1 through 12 on chalkboard and draw lines between numbers. Gather large gameboard with 12 frogs, 12 frogs, two dice, and copy of student gameboard. Optional: *Jumanji* and *Frog and Toad Are Friends*.

Part 1: Hop to the Pond—6 Frogs Race! (Grades K–3)

Modeling the Game with the Whole Class

1. Gather students in circle away from desks. Ask first graders what they know about dice. Examine large dice. Have second and third graders write letter describing dice. Have students read letters and record information about dice.

2. Show students large gameboard. Place frogs on the board and count, with students, how many frogs are racing. Ask students to predict which frog will get to pond first by a show of hands as you call each number.

3. Roll the die. Explain that the frog whose number corresponds to number on the top face of die can move one space. Pass the die one way round the circle and have children take turns rolling it. Let the children the other way round the circle the next child takes turns moving the proper frog forward one space.

4. During the game, ask questions as in text. Play until one frog wins. Ask more questions.

Playing Hop to the Pond with a Partner

1. Show student gameboard. Model how to set up and play game with a child partner. On each turn, have one person both roll the die and move the frog. Take turns doing this until everyone understands how to play with partner.

2. Explain that after they've played the game and have a winner, they'll come to the chalkboard. They'll write the number of the winning frog on a "post-it." Put "post-it" on chalkboard next to same number. Students can play game again.

3. Have students play game; circulate while they play. Assist with their "post-its."

4. When everyone has completed at least one game and posted results, collect game materials. Focus attention on chalkboard. Count and record how many "post-its" are next to each number. Write zero if a frog did not win any races. As in text, ask questions to interpret data. Resist temptation to explain data any further than students suggest. Let them play more to discover that all the frogs stand an equal chance of winning the game.

Part 2: Hop to the Pond—Now 12 Frogs Race! (Grades 1–3)

Modeling the Game with the Whole Class

1. Gather students in circle away from desks. Tell students now 6 more frogs are being added to game. Show new large gameboard. Place frogs on gameboard and count how many frogs are racing. Ask students to predict which frog will get to pond first by a show of hands as you call each number.

2. Explain that two dice will be used in this game. Roll pair of dice. Explain that the frog whose number corresponds to sum of dice can move one space. Model how to move the proper frog. Explain that you will move the frog in this first race as the students roll the dice.

3. Pass one die to each student beside you. Have these two students roll the dice. Have the class determine the sum and say which frog can move. Move the proper frog one space. Continue passing the dice around the circle, rolling them, determining the sum, and moving the proper frog.

4. After about eight rolls, ask questions as in text. Continue until each student has rolled one die. It is not important to finish the race, just to model how to use two dice and move the frog. Ask for more observations about the race.

Playing Hop to the Pond with a Partner

1. Show student gameboard. Choose a student partner. Model how to set up and play part of game with a partner. Place 12 frogs on the gameboard. Take turns rolling both dice. Find the sum together. The person who rolled the dice moves the proper frog. To be sure students understand, ask for a volunteer to review how to play.

2. Tell students that as in the first game, they'll write number of the winning frog on a "post-it" and place the "post-it" on the chalkboard next to the corresponding number.

3. Have students play game. Circulate while they play. Assist as necessary.

4. When all students have finished at least one game and posted results, collect materials. Focus attention on chalkboard. Count and record how many "post-its" are next to each number. Write zero if a frog did not win any races. As in text, ask questions to interpret data.

5. After just one round, students may not have answers. Resist temptation to explain data any further than students suggest. Let them play more to discover that certain frogs are more likely to win more than others.

6. If a student comes up with an important, accurate observation, allow her to explain her thinking to the group. By listening to students' thinking, you'll gain insight into their level of thinking. Proceed at their pace.

Button Template

Kindergarten Button Template

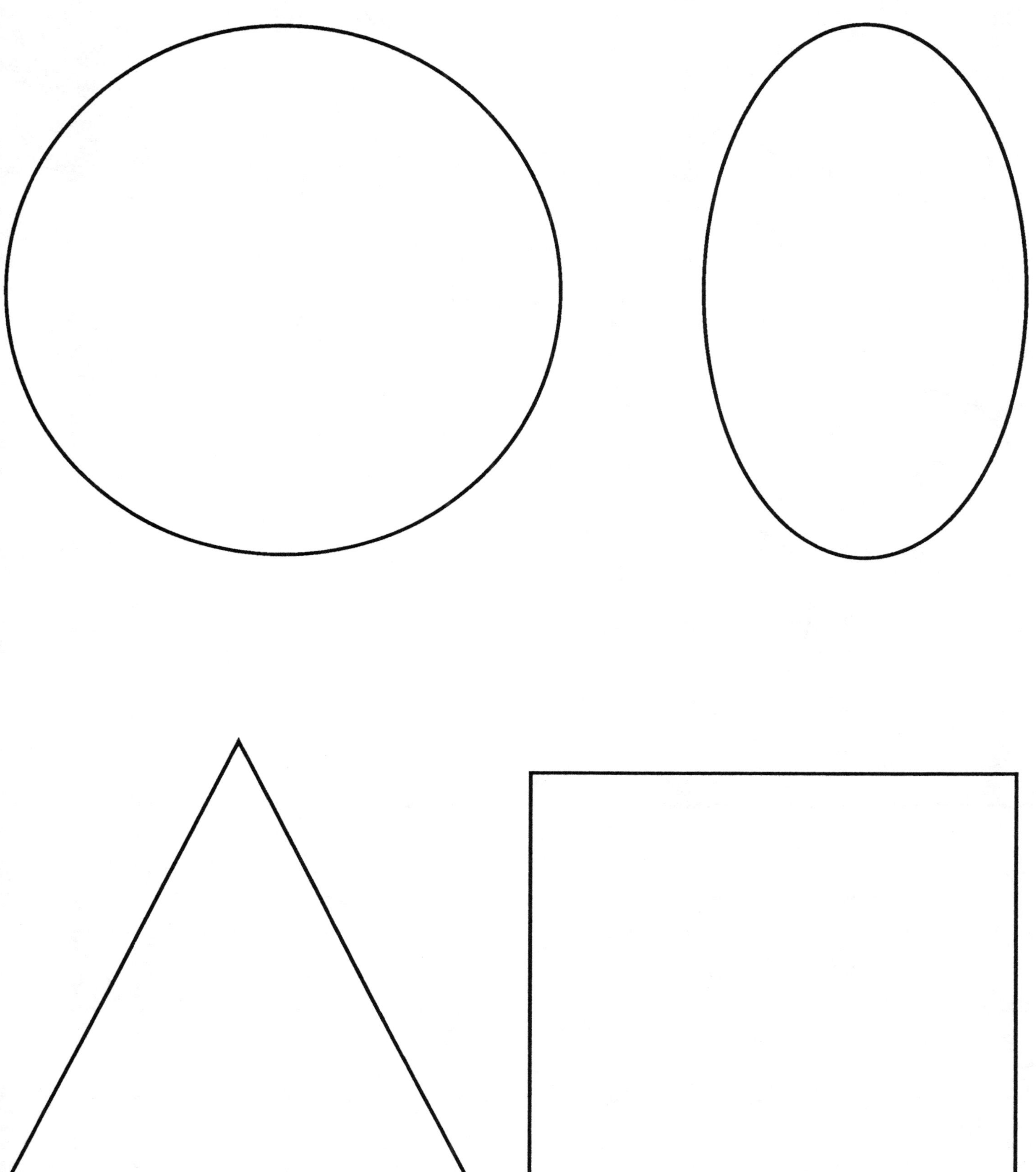

tens	ones

Hop To The Pond!

1

2

3

4

5

6

Hop To
1
2
3
4
5
6
1
2
3
4
5
6
1
2
3
4
5
6

The Pond!
7
8
9
10
11
12
7
8
9
10
11
12
7
8
9
10
11
12

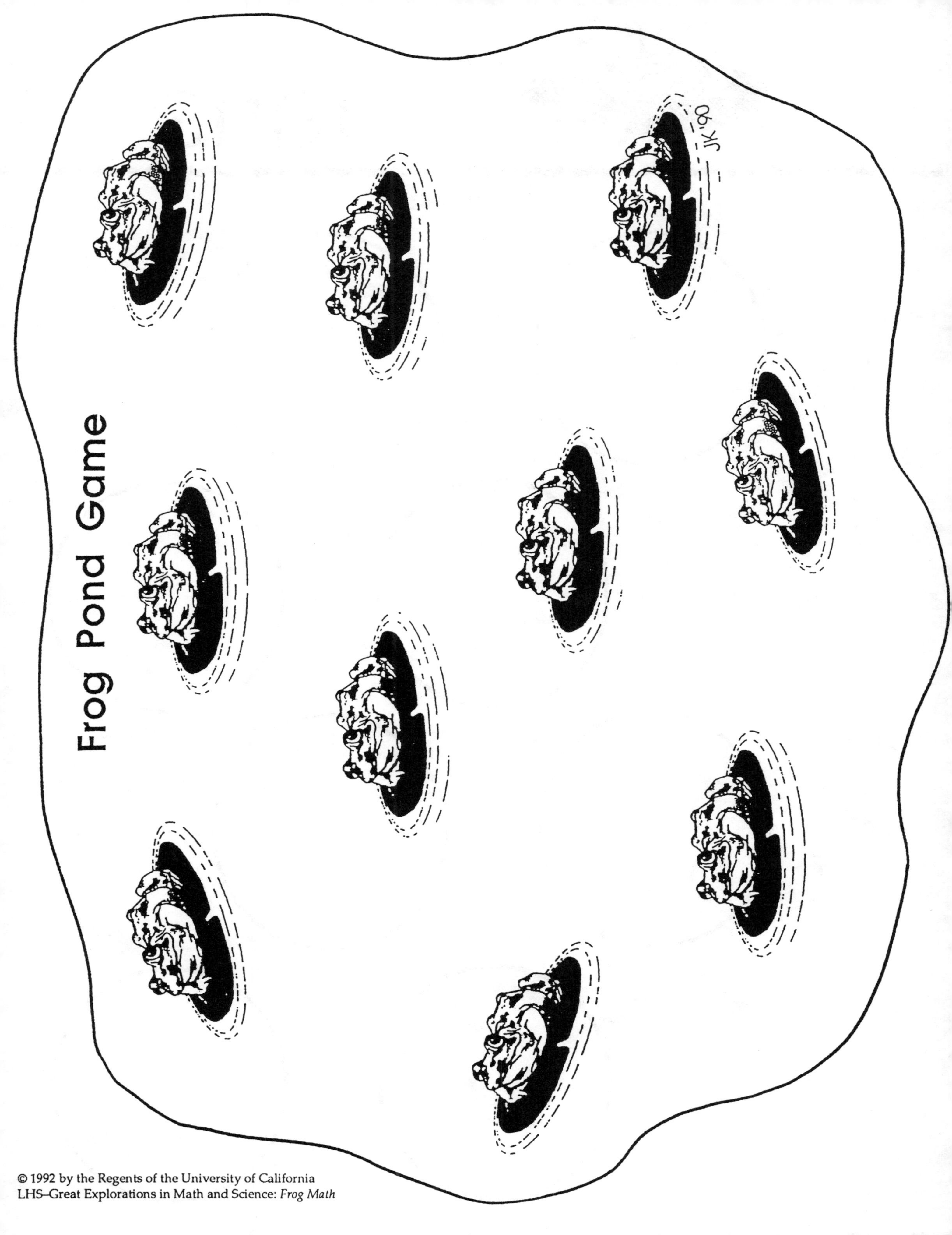
Frog Pond Game

tens

ones

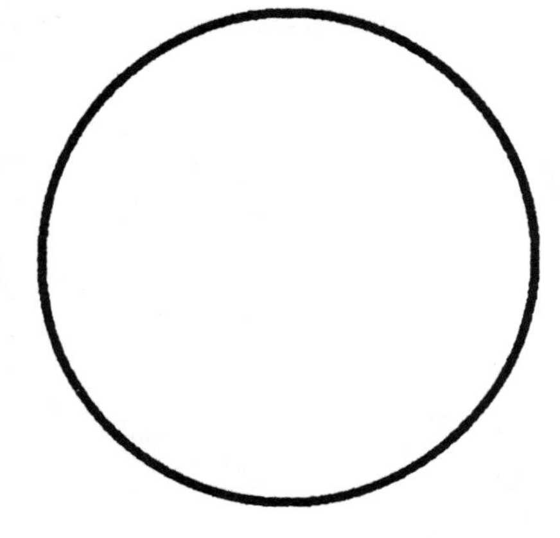

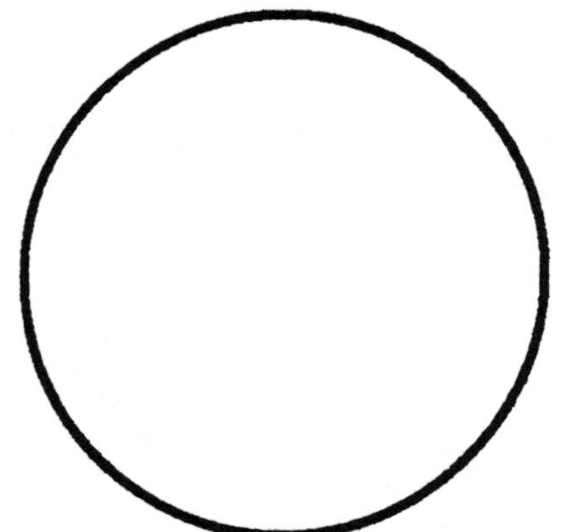

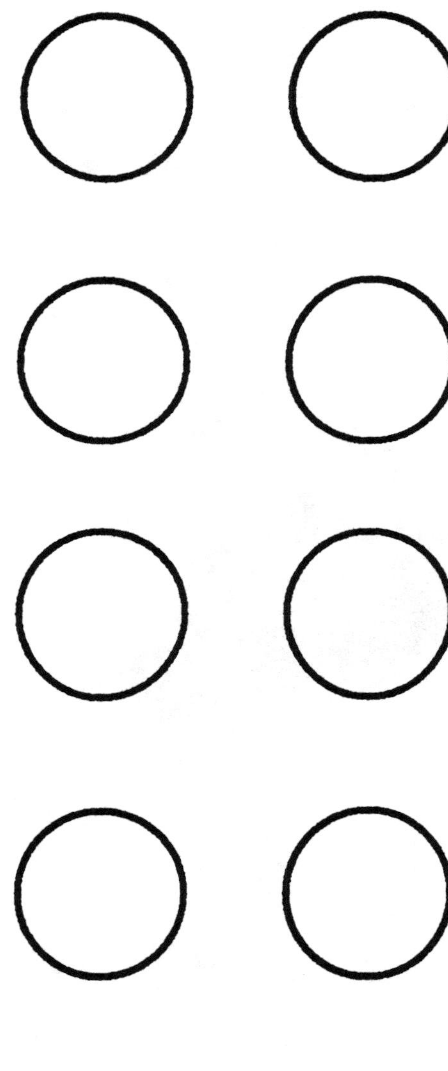

Frog Po

nd Game

Hop To The

Pond!
1
2
3
4
5
6

Hop To
1
2
3
4
5
6
1
2
3
4
5
6
1
2
3
4
5
6

The Pond!
7
8
9
10
11
12
7
8
9
10
11
12
7
8
9
10
11
12

ROLL ALL SIX

1. Guess how many times you need to throw the die before you see every number come up.

   Write down your guess: ☐

2. Now, throw the die and make a check mark for the number that comes up. Keep doing this until every number has come up.

3. Add up all the check marks. How close was your guess to this number?